Contents

Practice Test 1

Paper 1: Reading & Use of English

Part 1

1	C	3	D	5	B	7	A
2	A	4	B	6	C	8	A

Part 2

9	only	12	well	15	beyond
10	who	13	further	16	ever
11	What	14	During/Through		

Part 3

17	historically	21	disagreements
18	derivative/derivation	22	lucrative
19	activities	23	intellectuals
20	prosperous	24	specialising

Part 4

25 must/have to be taken into consideration

26 she had every chance of winning/she had a good chance of winning/she stood a good chance of winning

27 to spend all/the whole day answering

28 seems to have taken offence at

29 little prospect that we will have/of (our) having nice weather

30 a result of my promotion

Part 5

31	B	32	A	33	D	34	C	35	D	36	D

Part 6

37	G	39	E	41	H	43	F
38	D	40	B	42	A		

Part 7

44	B	46	C	48	D	50	A	52	D
45	B	47	A	49	D	51	C	53	B

Paper 2: Writing (Suggested Answers)

Part 1

The two texts look at the role of zoos in the modern world and question the effectiveness of the policies that zoos now follow in order to protect endangered species.

The first text acknowledges the important role that zoos play in trying to prevent the extinction of endangered species, which has involved the creation and development of the science of captive breeding. However, it doubts whether this policy can actually have any real effect on the survival prospects of endangered species.

The second text asks what the goals of modern zoos should be when promoting the welfare and conservation of animals. The text points out that one of the major flaws in captive breeding programmes as a conservation tool is that animals bred in captivity are unlikely to be released into the wild. One reason for this is that there are fewer and fewer natural habitats for them to be reintroduced into. The text suggests that, since captive breeding is extremely costly, resources would be better employed in protecting the natural habitats in which the animals thrive. It ends on an upbeat note with the observation that many zoos are now working to protect animals in their original wild habitats.

It is encouraging that zoos are now beginning to realise that they do have a role in helping to conserve the natural habitats of wild animals. While there is likely always to be a need to keep some animals in captivity, the main focus of species conservation ought to be on preserving species in the wild.

Part 2 – 2

The public's seemingly insatiable demand for the titillation of reality TV, where audiences can vicariously live the lives of the participants, has been answered with yet another new show, this time delving into the privileged lives of the offspring of the rich and famous. 'Brats!' follows the day to day lives of a group of friends whose parents are all multi-millionaires.

Even those amongst us who have tired of the whole over-exploited and exploitative format of reality TV will find it hard to resist the urge to look into these spoilt young people's lives. Their lives are so far removed from most people's that watching their interactions holds a great deal of fascination. Watching last night's opening episode I was both amused and horrified by the sense of entitlement, the arrogance and the brash tastelessness of this group of young people.

But I'm not sure the series will be able to hang onto my natural sense of curiosity for very long because the fact is that however you dress it up, the whole reality TV format is tired. We've seen it all before. I don't see how the show's producers can squeeze anything new out of the genre to hold our attention for very long. It might have helped if any of the participants were people we could somehow empathise with. Judging by last night's viewing, I would say this is unlikely from such a loathsome bunch of young adults. The name for the show was well chosen.

I'm sure the show won't be a complete flop as many people still retain an interest in watching these kinds of programmes. I can only surmise that this is due to some natural human instinct to be nosey about other people and the inherent enjoyment in talking about others behind their backs. But all told, the spark isn't really there anymore where reality TV is concerned.

Part 2 – 3

This report looks into the results of the recent renovation and development of our local town centre and what effect this has had on the local community.

The main development was the construction of a large shopping centre in the town centre. It is hoped this will help the economic regeneration of the town by encouraging more people from surrounding areas to visit. The new centre is well designed, attractive and has a large number of shops, eateries and other facilities, making it a convenient place to shop or indulge in other leisure activities. However, its popularity has come at the expense of many small independent shops that have now seen a sharp decline in profits.

One improvement which may help to restore the fortunes of small shops in the centre is the pedestrianisation of many of the streets, which has allowed for greater ease of movement for pedestrians and shoppers. It has also made visiting the town a much pleasanter and more relaxing experience now that traffic has been excluded from the area. The measure is a vast improvement on the way things were.

The same can also be said for the improvement in transport links. It is now a great deal more convenient to get into town by public transport than by private car. The centre is more accessible, especially for those, such as the elderly, who are unlikely to run a private car anyway. Even car owners in the area have recognised the benefits of decreased traffic and increased accessibility in the new system.

On the whole, the upgrade is likely to be very beneficial to the area by giving a much needed boost to the economy. While there has been a downturn in the fortunes of some local businesses due to the new shopping centre, hopefully this will be a spur to motivate these businesses to become more innovative in the future.

Part 2 – 4

Why it's Good to be Your Own Boss.

There's no doubt that being your own boss is a risky business, but one that can pay off, if you get it right. The key to doing well is to make sure, whatever you do, that it's something that has a strong selling point, either in goods or services.

In the future, and with a bit of capital from my parents, I hope to establish my own business in retail clothing. This is a business with a lot of potential but also one that can easily bomb. There are a number of factors involved in being a success in the retail clothing industry. First and foremost, you need to have an eye for style and choosing fashion ranges that will appeal to the demographic you are marketing your goods to. You also need to have premises in an area where they will be noticed and which is accessible to a high number of people. If you can pull all this together, it's a good business to be in because people love fashion and always want new clothes.

Owning your own business is extremely hard work because the hours are long and you are the one who is responsible for every aspect of the business. You basically have to be very good at every aspect of your business. That means being able to make the right decisions on how to make it profitable and knowing how to market your products and offer good service to customers. But for those who can mange all this, it can be very rewarding both emotionally and financially. There's a lot to be said for being in complete control of your own destiny.

For anyone hoping to go into business, it's a good idea to put the rose-tinted glasses down. Achieving success can be back-breaking work. But for those with nerves of steel, ambition and determination it is a goal that can be achieved.

Paper 3: Listening

Part 1

1 A	2 B	3 C	4 B	5 A	6 B

Part 2

7	world language	12	inherently
8	voyages (of discovery)	13	objective standards
9	(two) factors	14	(highly) complex
10	mother tongue	15	dependent
11	determine		

Part 3

16 D	17 B	18 D	19 A	20 D

5

Part 4

21	C	23	A	25	D	27	B	29	C
22	F	24	E	26	F	28	G	30	E

Practice Test 2

Paper 1: Reading & Use of English

Part 1

1	C	3	B	5	D	7	D
2	B	4	A	6	C	8	B

Part 2

9	them	12	results	15	such
10	were	13	While	16	However
11	then	14	other		

Part 3

17	respectively	21	agricultural
18	characterised	22	considerably
19	normally	23	transmission
20	resultant/resulting	24	Researchers

Part 4

25 is constantly finding fault with
26 can hardly wait to start
27 to be binding it must be signed by
28 takes it for granted (that) I will let/allow/permit
29 thanks to him/his encouragement that I
30 difficult/hard to come to terms with

Part 5

31	D	32	B	33	D	34	A	35	B	36	A

Part 6

37	C	39	G	41	H	43	B
38	A	40	D	42	F		

Part 7

44	A	46	D	48	D	50	B	52	D
45	C	47	B	49	A	51	B	53	C

Paper 2: Writing (Suggested Answers)

Part 1

The sedentary and repetitive nature of modern working life has caused a large number of employees to experience health problems, most notably the pain and discomfort associated with Repetitive Strain Injury. The costs are great for those that fall victim to these health problems but, as these two texts highlight, employers, companies and the wider economy all suffer as well through compensation costs and loss of productivity.

As both texts observe, these problems can be solved if ergonomic adjustments are made to the working environment. Such changes may include providing staff with better chairs, cutting out glare from the windows and making sure that the temperature is optimal. As well as changes to the environment, changes will usually need to be made to the working patterns and habits of the employees. Do they take breaks or change task often enough? Are they sitting correctly?

Although both texts acknowledge the role that bad posture and repetition often plays in the development of work-related health conditions, I was disappointed that neither text emphasises the importance of providing workers with training as part of the solution. I believe it is essential that office workers have a good understanding of what constitutes correct posture and realise the importance of taking regular breaks from repetitive tasks. They should also be encouraged to take responsibility, along with the company, for their health and well-being. If something in their environment is problematic, they should not feel hesitant about raising the issue and seeking a solution.

To sum up, as well as ergonomic and environmental changes to offices, ergonomic training should be as routine as learning how to use the company's databases.

Part 2 – 2

Art Nouveau is a small bijou hotel that has opened up in the centre of town to cater to both tourists and business clientele. The hotel is favourably situated close to Stanley Park and the building is a recently renovated 19th century mansion. I booked a room for one night to see if it is as good as it looks in the glossy brochure advertising the hotel.

The building has been beautifully renovated with many of the original features, such as intricate plasterwork on the ceiling, retained. The furniture in the lobby is antique but comfortable and gives the place a homely atmosphere. Each of the rooms in the hotel is decorated according to an individual theme. I stayed in the room known as Victorian Glory, which is full of Victorian antiques and the furnishings are in rich, dark colours. It looks like a Pre-Raphaelite interior come to life.

The staff at the hotel are very friendly and service is impeccable. The small restaurant in the hotel is run very efficiently and is a pleasant place to have dinner whether you are staying in the hotel or not. It provides good, well-made food and pleasant service. But do be prepared to pay more than usual here. Neither the restaurant, nor the rooms are particularly cheap. I wouldn't class them as eye-wateringly expensive but a little more than usual. But if you factor in the quality of the service provided, then there's little to argue about, to be honest.

All in all, I think this is one of the better hotels in the area. It's a warm and inviting place to stay and the décor makes it a cut above the usual boring, sterile hotel experience. Service and staff cannot be faulted and although the hotel is a bit on the pricey side, I can honestly say that you get what you pay for.

Part 2 – 3

Can you imagine what kind of world we will be leaving to our children and grandchildren if we do nothing to help protect the environment now? Around the world, the environment is in crisis and it's up to all of us to turn the situation around without delay. And the amount of effort needed to help is really not much at all. All you really need to change is the way you think.

What do I mean by that? The problem is that people don't think about the consequences of their actions. Leaving one light on might not make much difference to your bill but thousands of lights left on, thousands of taps left dripping, all add up to a lot of waste. So every time you do something try to imagine what the consequences of that action would be if you were a thousand people instead of just one.

That's the simplest change you can make. But you could also get involved with some of the environmental groups in your area that are actively campaigning on behalf of the environment. With just a few hours of volunteer work a week, you can make a huge difference. There are all sorts of different groups and they all focus on something different, whether that be conservation, campaigning or education. Find what suits you best and get involved.

The consequences of apathy are just too serious to be ignored. If we don't all work together as a community to ensure the protection of our environment we will all pay a heavy price in the very near future. All it takes to change the world is a little willing.

It's up to all of us.

Part 2 – 4

I am writing this report, at the request of senior management, to analyse the results of recent renovation works on the company premises and to evaluate their effects on worker productivity and relations with clients, as well as make any necessary recommendations.

During renovations all the old fittings and furnishings were ripped out, non-supporting walls were removed to enlarge rooms and offices, and windows were enlarged to let in more light. New modern minimalist furniture has replaced the outdated style of furniture the premises had previously.

The overall effect of the renovations has been to make the premises seem much larger, more airy and with a great deal more natural light. The atmosphere feels cleaner, leaner and more modern. Because the main rooms are now bigger, more work stations can be fitted into the main rooms. Also management offices seem less cluttered now that they have more streamlined furnishings.

This seems to have had a good effect on the work force. The very atmosphere of the building does a lot to promote efficiency and this has been reflected in the general upbeat feeling and improvement in morale and productivity in all departments since renovation work was concluded.

There is no doubt that this has also had a beneficial effect on the impression the company gives to clients, which has been reflected in an upturn in contracts in the past six months. The renovations have not only made doing business easier in terms of more available and better utilised space, but in terms of enhancing our image to outsiders.

It is now imperative that the company maintains the momentum that the renovations have helped inspire. Keeping the workplace efficient is as much about managing and utilising space efficiently as it is about managing people. The premises should be kept as clean and clutter free as possible in order to make the most of the space.

Paper 3: Listening

Part 1

1 B	2 B	3 C	4 C	5 A	6 B

Part 2

7	redundancy money	12	disillusioned
8	spectacular	13	sake
9	self-sufficient	14	satisfying
10	part-time employment	15	resilient
11	(extensive) garden		

Part 3

| 16 C | 17 C | 18 A | 19 B | 20 B |

Part 4

| 21 B | 23 H | 25 C | 27 D | 29 E |
| 22 G | 24 A | 26 G | 28 A | 30 C |

Practice Test 3
Paper 1: Reading & Use of English

Part 1

| 1 C | 3 B | 5 C | 7 B |
| 2 D | 4 C | 6 A | 8 A |

Part 2

| 9 both | 11 to/in | 13 were/is | 15 either |
| 10 which | 12 with | 14 no | 16 over |

Part 3

17 uncertainty	21 settlements
18 domestication	22 gracefully
19 disposition	23 retractable
20 researchers	24 exemplary

Part 4

25 fell short of my expectations even though/ considering that
26 is no excuse for being so
27 can be depended on/upon to get lost
28 rarely takes notice of/takes little notice of
29 is forbidden to enter this area without
30 a full understanding of the problem will there

Part 5

| 31 D | 32 B | 33 A | 34 C | 35 C | 36 B |

Part 6

| 37 F | 39 G | 41 A | 43 C |
| 38 D | 40 H | 42 E | |

Part 7

| 44 E | 46 B | 48 C | 50 E | 52 C |
| 45 D | 47 A | 49 D | 51 B | 53 A |

Paper 2: Writing (Suggested Answers)

Part 1

These texts discuss humour in different countries. The first takes the view that there are fundamental differences in the sense of humour of different countries, while the second implies that good comedy can be appreciated by people of any nationality and culture.

The first text gives 'The Office' as an example which shows the differences in the humour of Britain and America. It observes that the American version is far more optimistic than the bleak British original, and that although both versions portray a blundering boss in charge of a dysfunctional office, the boss in the American version does have some positive characteristics. The writer takes these differences as evidence of a deep cultural divide in the humour of the two countries.

The second text, however, emphasises the universality of humour by showing how national stereotypes about humour can be false. According to the findings of a research project on jokes, Germans do not lack a sense of humour but actually tend to have a better sense of humour than people of other nationalities. The writer also provides examples of American TV shows which make heavy use of irony to show that it is not true that Americans do not understand irony. The writer clearly believes that the stereotypes are outdated and that people of different nationalities have a similar sense of humour.

I agree with the second text as in my experience humour often crosses cultural boundaries. I enjoy watching foreign comedy just as much as comedy from my home country. The writer of the first text relies on one example to confirm his pre-existing opinion, and in this way he is only reinforcing, and not questioning, inaccurate stereotypes.

Part 2 – 2

The purpose of this report is to assess the success of the new measures introduced at the leisure centre to boost the number of new members who join in activities at the centre.

The first of the new measures that have been introduced is a change to pricing. In the past there were flat rate prices either per month or for a year. Now we have introduced payments for 1, 3, 6 or 12 month periods with reductions in price for the longer membership contracts. Discounts have also been introduced for couples, families, senior citizens and groups of over 10 people in order to make the pricing more attractive to a larger group.

Furthermore, the centre has now extended its opening times to remain open later in the evenings by two hours, so the centre now closes at 10pm. During the weekends there has been no change in the Saturday opening times of 10am – 6pm, but the same opening times have now been added for Sundays when the centre was previously closed.

The final measures introduced have been some changes to the range of activities offered. Now exercise classes are offered to groups or individual members can hire their own personal trainer for sessions. A variety of exercise classes are directed at mothers and children together, and there are also new classes aimed at older age groups.

The results of these new measures have been astounding. In the three months since they were introduced, membership has risen by 28%. In consequence of this it seems fair to say that flexible pricing, flexible opening times and directed exercise classes are popular with the public, and we should therefore look into what other creative measures the centre could introduce in the future to boost membership even further.

Part 2 – 3

In many ways, the Second World War was a defining moment in British History and the success of the allied forces has contributed to the national outlook of the countries that were members of the victorious armies. In Britain, many people have learned the history of this war through a documentary series called The World at War, which has been running on repeat for forty years. Although the series is generally excellent, it has also contributed to myth making and jingoism.

There is no doubt the series was very well made and highly informative. The World at War has helped generations of young people understand what happened in the Second World War and why. The use of original film footage and excellent narration has helped bring alive the history of the war in a way no book ever could. Without this programme a large number of British people may never have understood the significance of this war and why it should never be forgotten.

One effect of the constant repeats of the series over the years is that it has contributed to the idea that only the countries that were on the winning side were of any value. This has helped build a myth of the superiority of the people from countries in the allied forces and that there was something wrong with those from the axis forces. The net result of this is continuing jingoism about the war.

The series has been a part of my life since my childhood and is a part of the culture of my country. While, on the one hand, I admire it as a brilliantly made documentary series, I also feel that it has, through constant repetition, reinforced a myth about the Second World War whereby the victorious side were all good and the losing one all evil. I do not think this is conducive to good relations between all nations of the world.

Part 2 – 4

Dear Editor,

I read this week's article on cyberbullying with great interest because in my opinion it is a problem that is not getting enough attention.

The internet is a very powerful tool that can easily be used in a destructive way. Bullies have always caused great distress and harm to their victims but, by targeting their victims on the internet, they are able to reach new parts of their victims' lives in front of a much greater audience. A bully can now hurt his victim when he is at home, a place where he should feel safe, by writing a hurtful message that will appear on his screen, and that message can easily be read by thousands of people in a short space of time.

Although I have not experienced cyberbullying myself, I am very aware of the damage it can cause. After one of my friends at school broke up with her boyfriend, he put unflattering pictures of her on the internet along with unkind comments and hateful lies. He sent this to all of his friends, and soon the whole school had seen it. Sometimes people she did not even know would recognise her and laugh at her.

Cyberbullying is not an easy problem to solve because it is very hard to control what people put onto the internet. However, there are some steps that could be taken to improve the situation. Firstly young people, teachers and parents should be made aware of cyberbullying so that they can recognise the signs and do something to stop it. Secondly, there should be strict laws and punishments for bullies that continue even after they have been warned. Lastly, internet companies should take a greater role in stopping cyberbullying and should be able to identify and remove offending content quickly.

I hope your magazine will continue to raise awareness of this serious problem.

Yours faithfully,

Paper 3: Listening

Part 1

1 B   2 C   3 C   4 A   5 B   6 A

Part 2

7 cramped
8 enough space
9 surprising
10 weight is concentrated
11 virtually
12 declined
13 fin
14 gives birth
15 vulnerable fish

Part 3

16 B   17 C   18 C   19 D   20 A

Part 4

21 B   23 D   25 F   27 A   29 C
22 H   24 G   26 E   28 G   30 B

Practice Test 4

Paper 1: Reading & Use of English

Part 1

1 D   3 D   5 C   7 D
2 B   4 A   6 A   8 B

Part 2

9 were
10 after
11 nothing
12 some
13 without
14 like
15 former
16 while

Part 3

17 revitalise
18 partnership
19 notably
20 acclaim
21 theatrical
22 lyricists
23 dissimilar
24 operatic

Part 4

25 unlikely to meet the approval of the council/the council's approval
26 make it impossible for the bank to grant/give
27 arrange for the immediate delivery of
28 no account must you forget
29 failure (to succeed) was a (direct) consequence of
30 accept/take the blame for

Part 5

31 C   32 B   33 B   34 B   35 A   36 B

Part 6

37 H   39 G   41 F   43 D
38 B   40 C   42 A

Part 7

44 E   46 D   48 E   50 A   52 A
45 B   47 C   49 C   51 B   53 D

Paper 2: Writing (Suggested Answers)

Part 1

Both the texts look at the problems caused by dyslexia and what kind of strategies can be used to help both children and adults who have been diagnosed as dyslexic.

The first text discusses some of the problems that dyslexic children face. Not only may they have trouble with literacy skills but dyslexia can also affect them in other ways, such as affecting their memory, for instance. It is argued that dyslexic children should not be pushed too hard in a learning environment and that they can make good progress. But those dyslexic children who are not diagnosed face discrimination in education and may end up rejecting it out of hand. The key to helping dyslexic children is to make the classroom a safe and motivating environment for all children.

The second text also looks at ways of helping adults who have been diagnosed as dyslexic in adulthood. The writer points out that in order for dyslexic adults to get the right kind of help they are likely to need a proper assessment of their dyslexia. The text also points out how the simple fact that dyslexic adults have had a proper diagnosis can help them to come to terms with their condition and to reevaluate their earlier learning experiences. In this text the emphasis is on the best way to ensure that dyslexic adults reach their full potential.

Overall, both texts make clear that the key to improving the literacy and other learning skills of dyslexic adults and children is an encouraging environment.

Part 2 – 2

Looking back at the formative experiences of my childhood which had the most influence on who I have become as an adult, I think the seminal ones were to do with the fact that we moved around the world so much in my childhood.

For the first eight years of my life my parents travelled extensively due to my father's work in telecommunications. So I lived in the United States, Africa, and the Caribbean as a young child. In some ways, it was quite a disruptive start to my life, as no sooner had we settled than we were off again. I must have changed schools half a dozen times in the first few years of my education. But in some ways this disruption has helped me to cope with change in adult life. I don't feel quite so unsettled by change as perhaps those who come from more stable backgrounds do.

Another benefit of my early travel experiences is that living in other cultures and with people from other races helped to make me more tolerant of others from a very early age. I have always been part of a multicultural world and so it is nothing new or strange to me. As a result, I'm always willing and eager to learn about other cultures and enjoy trying new things out, such as different kinds of food. Unlike more insular people, I do not feel threatened by the presence of people from other cultures.

On the whole, I think I was extremely lucky to have such an exciting childhood and while it meant, in some ways, that my early existence was somewhat unsettled, it also meant that I gained a breadth of experience of the world that many of my contemporaries did not.

Part 2 – 3

This report is to assess the suitability of local beauty spots and facilities for promotion in order to develop both summer and winter tourism in the area.

One area that has always been popular with locals is the Sudbury canal and lock, located just outside the east side of the town. This is a highly attractive area surrounded by farmland. The part of the canal and lock just outside of the village of Sudbury has some pleasant village inns with restaurants, so visitors have easy access to good facilities. The tow path of the canal is suitable for walks and canal barges can be hired at Sudbury lock to take trips down the canal. It's also possible to hire canal barges for long periods for those who would like to have accommodation on a barge.

The area surrounding Peak's Crag is suitable for hiking and mountaineering in both the summer and winter. It's an area that would also be suited to development of a ski resort with winter chalets. At the moment, the area has cottages for rent and a few small, but very good, country farmhouse style hotels. Most of them are quite upmarket and the restaurants have a very good reputation.

Another area suitable for tourist development is Begley beach, the three mile stretch of coast on the west side of the town. Although there has not been much tourist development in the area, it is a very charming seaside locale. In summer the sea is good for bathing and the cliffs to the north of the beach are good for walking and have spectacular sea views. The area is ripe for development but, at the moment, affordable Bed and Breakfast rooms are the main accommodation near the beach.

To conclude, all three areas are suitable for promotion for summer visitors and Peak's Crag is an area that could be very attractive to winter visitors as well.

Part 2 – 4

It's been a long wait but Kingswood has finally acquired a branch of the Golden Goose restaurant chain. So, overcome with excitement about this major event, I decided to splash out and take a friend for dinner this week and I thought some of you might like to hear about it.

The décor is sleek and modern with cool colours and simple, indeed spartan, furniture. The floors are tiled and the walls too. So, it does look super clean. The music played was a mixture of jazz and modern classical, which also added to the hip image of the restaurant and this was reflected by the fact that most of the clientele were the arty bohemian crowd.

I can make no complaints about the service, which is fast and efficient. I had expected, as it happens all too often in upmarket establishments, that the serving staff would be rude and stand offish and behave as though everyone dining there were beneath them. But not a bit of it. The staff are very knowledgeable and happy to give advice about dishes on the menu and what to choose to go with them from the wine list.

The one disappointment was the food. And, of course, it's the food that needs to stand out at any restaurant charging from eighty pounds and up for two people. It's not that the food was bad. In fact, it was relatively decent and well cooked. It simply lacked flair and there was nothing that marked it out from the food in any decent local bistro, which charges half the price of the Golden Goose.

In the end, the fact that the food wasn't quite up to scratch means I'm unlikely to visit again. It's a lovely place and the staff are marvellous but if I'm going to pay an arm and a leg for dinner, I really do want it to be special.

Paper 3: Listening

Part 1
1 C		2 B		3 C		4 C		5 B		6 C

Part 2
7	supernatural beings	12	slow and expensive
8	in its heyday	13	burial
9	inscriptions	14	high status
10	soldiers	15	digging
11	onion		

Part 3

16 B   17 B   18 D   19 C   20 A

Part 4

21 E   23 C   25 D   27 H   29 C
22 G   24 A   26 G   28 E   30 A

Practice Test 5

Paper 1: Reading & Use of English

Part 1

1 C   3 A   5 B   7 D
2 D   4 B   6 C   8 B

Part 2

9 never   11 those   13 latter   15 unlike
10 there   12 what   14 little/no 16 to

Part 3

17 indebted   21 collaborator
18 unstintingly   22 unflagging
19 necessitated   23 recognition
20 enabled   24 exceptionally

Part 4

25 is intent on becoming
26 insisted he had no knowledge of
27 was still no sign of her friends by/at
28 to have decided against buying
29 has little/no flair for – doesn't have a/much (of a) flair for
30 am always short of money by

Part 5

31 B   32 C   33 C   34 D   35 C   36 C

Part 6

37 D   39 B   41 G   43 C
38 A   40 H   42 F

Part 7

44 B   46 B   48 D   50 D   52 C
45 C   47 D   49 A   51 B   53 A

Paper 2: Writing (Suggested Answers)

Part 1

In recent times there have been some new developments in the way people are organising their communities, such as the kind of housing in them and what social effects that has.

Co-housing is a new way of organising communities that has, at its core, a belief in community. The idea is in some ways rather utopian, in that a certain amount of commitment is necessary from all members of the community – members are expected to help design the community and maintain it. What makes this idea utopian in my view is the idea that the organisation of these communities is non-hierarchical, which is something I believe has never been truly achieved in any society. But there is no doubt that the idea of having all members of a community actively participating in it is a laudable one.

Social housing is another sector that has seen a desire to make communities more closely-knit. Councils are now rethinking the policies of the past that saw people thrown into run down high-rise estates that were the cause of much social breakdown. Now the emphasis is on low rise dwellings and sustainable design that has a lower impact on the environment. This sea change in policy is due, in part, to working with tenants and making sure their wants and needs were catered for.

On the whole, many of the new ideas about dealing with housing needs in modern times are very positive, as they are more centred on community and environmental considerations than in the past. Some ideas may be a little too optimistic but the fact that people are changing their communities for the better is a positive thing.

Part 2 – 2

This report analyses the data relating to the amount of money raised by the organisation in the past 6 months, where it was decided to distribute the funds and under what criteria grants were given.

The bulk of the monies collected was as a result of this year's Christmas appeal that was promoted through local branches of the organisation as well as other community centres. As usual, we were strongly supported by other local community organisations in our fund-raising drive, especially the Women's Institute. The rest of the funds were collected by a variety of initiatives including: collection boxes, sponsored activities and local fetes and jumble sales.

This year it was decided by the executive committee that the funds raised should be given to local charities rather than large national ones. It was felt that national charities are much more likely to already have a lot of support whilst local charities are struggling to survive.

The main beneficiaries were those aid organisations that it was felt could do the most good for local communities at a time when the local community has suffered adverse effects from the current economic downturn. The organisation that received the biggest donation of ten thousand pounds was the Everly Centre for Disabled Children, which recently suffered a loss of government funding. The rest of the funds were divided between the Compton Community Workshop for the Unemployed and the local homeless shelter.

On the whole, the fund raising drive was a major success and one we hope can be repeated in the remainder of this year.

Part 2 – 3

In this day and age few could imagine living without electricity and petrol, and the machines and gadgets these energy forms allow us to use. But let us imagine what our daily lives would be like without them.

The first thing I do in the morning is jump in the shower and then put the kettle on for a cup of coffee, before running out the door to catch a bus to work. In the 19th century, the first thing I would have had to do is light a fire to heat water to wash in and to make a hot drink. There were no buses then and people simply walked to work.

Now, I work in an office with computers but if I'd been born in the 19th century, I would have been lucky to get a job in a factory. At the time Britain was at the forefront of the industrial revolution and the first machines were being used in industry. But in those days, the machines were noisy enough to make you deaf and very dangerous to work with. There were no health and safety regulations then.

Then after your shift and a long walk home, there was no television to watch and there was still more work to do, like cooking food on an open fire. There was no central heating and rooms were permanently cold in winter. If you became ill there were no medicines to help you. You were either healthy enough to pull through or you died. Life was very harsh indeed.

We often forget just how much easier our lives are compared to people in the past. Nothing was easy for them. Not even the simplest task like making a cup of tea. And some things, like the lack of basic medical care, meant that life was often very brief indeed. I'm certainly glad I live in the 21st century. How about you?

Part 2 – 4

Dear Sir,

I see that your newspaper is still advertising the Trigham Holiday company on its pages. I recently booked a holiday through them, renting a villa on the Amalfi coast. While I feel that the holiday company is not to blame for most of the problems my family and I encountered, I think they could do more to help travellers avoid some problems that, with a little more information available, would be wholly avoidable.

The villa we rented was lovely and in a very beautiful area. However, the maid service that was supposed to be daily was not up to scratch, as one maid appeared for a perfunctory five minutes a day and we were forced to clean the villa ourselves while on holiday. I think the company needs to do more to ensure the maid service does what it is paid to do. There don't appear to be enough checks and balances on the agency supplying the tour company with service staff.

Another service we were encouraged to use was a food delivery service. It delivered high quality delicatessen and supermarket food but the charges were exorbitant and it is much better to shop in the local area yourself. The tour company should make that clear. Another thing I wouldn't recommend is using local taxis. The drivers appear to think that foreign visitors have money to throw away. I would recommend that travellers hire a car rather than rely on taxis that have no meter and so simply charge whatever they want.

Although most of the problems were not directly the fault of the tour company, I think they could do more to inform visitors of potential problems. I would be interested to hear if any other readers have had similar problems with the company.

Yours faithfully,
Catherine Pritchard

Paper 3: Listening

Part 1

1 C	2 A	3 B	4 B	5 B	6 A

Part 2

7	living things	12	earliest inhabitants
8	symbolic content	13	female
9	passed down (orally)	14	male
10	supreme beings	15	clay tablets
11	virtuous life		

Part 3

16 C   17 B   18 D   19 C   20 A

Part 4

21 F	23 H	25 E	27 G	29 B
22 D	24 B	26 E	28 F	30 D

Practice Test 6
Paper 1: Reading & Use of English

Part 1

1 D	3 A	5 B	7 D
2 B	4 C	6 C	8 B

Part 2

9 and/or	12 much	15 already
10 back	13 Consequently	16 number
11 in	14 when	

Part 3

17 breathtaking	21 permeable
18 foregoing	22 traction
19 irrespective	23 substantially
20 priorities	24 lightened

Part 4

25 either side to agree on/accept the proposed solutions
26 injury is due to (it) trying/its attempt
27 must/will (have to) be demolished to make way
28 you cast your mind back
29 he had never gone back on his word/promises
30 was responsible for drawing up a contract between

Part 5

31 C   32 B   33 A   34 A   35 C   36 B

Part 6

37 D	39 G	41 B	43 E
38 A	40 C	42 H	

Part 7

44 C	46 A	48 D	50 A	52 D
45 D	47 C	49 B	51 C	53 B

Paper 2: Writing (Suggested Answers)

Part 1

There is no doubt that in recent years there has been a rise in the number of people taking part in extreme sports. Both texts examine the inherent dangers and consequences of taking part in these kinds of sports.

On the one hand, it is argued that the increase in participation in dangerous, extreme sports is putting an unnecessary strain on health and rescue services. The writer comes to the conclusion that there should be some restrictions on dangerous sports. The inherent problem with this argument is that there are many sports that can cause serious injury without being classed as extreme, so it would be unfair to penalise only some sports.

The second text raises the fact that the danger of extreme sports has been exaggerated and also compares the cost of treating a few extreme sports injuries with the cost of treating very large numbers of injuries from other sports which occur because so many people take part in them. The final comparison is with the number of people killed in traffic accidents, which is extremely high, yet no one would dream of suggesting cars be banned.

It does seem that many of the arguments around the dangers of sports are based on emotional factors rather than statistical evidence. In the end, it is likely that the less dangerous sports are the ones that actually cost health services the most because of the high number of participants. Extreme sports may be dangerous to participants but the low number of people doing them means that they are not a significant strain on resources.

Part 2 – 2

This report is on the results of research into the best option for developing the site of a disused factory.

The first option is to turn the whole site into a park. On the one hand, there is always a case to be made for increasing the number of green spaces in the town. However, the cost in this case would be very prohibitive. It would be expensive to demolish and clear the site and also to landscape the site from scratch. The town already has two large parks for recreation.

Another option would be to turn the site into an adventure playground. In many ways, the site is perfect for this kind of development. The cost of creating an adventure playground is not prohibitive in itself. However, it would be the cost of staffing and running the playground that would be a drain on the council budget. Staff wages and running costs would need to be subsidised via a high entrance fee, which would discourage users.

The final option is to develop the site for commercial use for small businesses to rent as workshops. The cost of redevelopment would be low and would be recouped via rents. Also it would help to encourage small businesses in the area. The only real disadvantage is that the site is quite far from the centre and businesses may need some incentives to rent from the site at first.

In conclusion, I would recommend the redevelopment of the site as workshops for small businesses as this would be a low cost project with economic benefits to the town. Both the park and adventure playground would cost more than they are likely to return in usefulness to the community as a whole.

Part 2 – 3

Although there is a wide range of films I enjoy going to the cinema to see, there are films I really enjoy and ones I don't, even within one particular genre. It depends on how well the film is actually made.

One of my favourite films is 'Kill Bill' directed by Quentin Tarantino. Although this film has a lot of violence in it, some of which is quite graphic, I don't feel it is gratuitous violence, as it is a cartoon way of depicting it. It's clear that the violence in the film is deliberately over the top and deliberately unrealistic. Besides which, the plot, script, acting and cinematography are so good that the violence is a small aspect of the film as a whole. The film is a fable, a fairy story and an enjoyable and even comic tribute to Japanese films.

Another director who has been influenced by Asian cinema is Martin Scorsese. His film 'The Departed' was simply a remake of a classic Hong Kong police drama, 'Infernal Affairs.' 'The Departed' was a huge disappointment to me, as it did not enhance the original film and, in places, it was nothing more than a direct copy of it, even down to camera shots. This film, despite being a very poor copy of a really good Asian film, is, inexplicably, the only film that Scorsese has won an Oscar for.

Tarantino's film is excellent, and, although it uses many of the conceits and ideas of Asian cinema, it is still a distinctive and original film. Scorsese's film is a copy that tries to make it look like as though his Hollywood direction was original when it was, in fact, wholly derivative.

Part 2 – 4

The news that the town is going to use part of East Park to develop a zoo and an aquarium is great. What isn't so great, is the news that funds for the project will be raised through the exploitation of performing animals.

It's one thing to keep animals in captivity. Zoos and aquariums serve many purposes, such as research into wildlife, protection of endangered species and education. Zoos are one of the first places that I learned about wildlife from. Going to a zoo as a child was an awe-inspiring experience and that embedded within me a desire to learn more about the animal kingdom. That same fascination is inspired by visits to aquariums too. Zoos and aquariums are the only places that some children will ever see a real live wild animal and it's important to make sure all future generations have an interest in protecting wildlife.

However, circuses and marine parks with performing animals are another subject entirely. I believe that they are cruel, as wild animals are not meant to be trained. They are also exploitative in that they make profit for the organisations owning the performing animals and none of that money goes back into improving the welfare of wild animals. Making wild animals perform is an affront to the dignity of the animal and it is a poor reflection on us to see that kind of humiliation of proud wild animals as entertainment.

In short, it is marvellous that a zoo and aquarium will be developed in our town. Unfortunately, I cannot agree that the way to fund the project is through the exploitation of performing animals. I think other methods of raising money could be found without adding to the cruelty of making animals perform as entertainment.

Paper 3: Listening

Part 1
1 C   2 B   3 A   4 B   5 B   6 A

Part 2
7   common and classical
8   medication
9   visual disturbances
10 very confused
11 stroke
12 excruciatingly painful
13 trigger
14 relieved
15 ferocious

Part 3
16 B   17 D   18 C   19 A   20 C

Part 4
21 C   23 A   25 D   27 F   29 C
22 B   24 H   26 D   28 A   30 H

Practice Test 1 – Paper 4 Speaking

Part 2

Stage 1 (Suggested Answer)

A: Let's start with picture 2. He looks like a very affectionate father, doesn't he?

B: Yes, he does. They're probably going out somewhere, so he's making sure his little son is nice and warm. Maybe the little boy wants to go to the playground or a park?

A: It's quite likely, you know how children love running around outdoors. It looks like they live in a city, no trees, no lawn. It's not exactly the best environment for children to play in.

B: I agree, city living is a problem, especially for little children. Locked up in small apartments with no gardens, or a tiny yard. Playing out in the fresh air is very important for children. It seems that Dad already knows this. So that's why he's braving the cold. But on the other hand, maybe Dad is taking the little one to a day care centre. With both parents working nowadays, children start their schooling very young.

A: Yes, that's right. This could be part of their daily routine. Let's move on to picture 4. Doesn't the old lady look happy?

B: She certainly does. She seems very happy and content crocheting or knitting something. I'm not sure what it is, a shawl? Anyway, it's a nice, bright yellow. She's probably making something for herself or her grandchildren, or maybe for a school fair.

A: Yes. Who knows? Of course her way of life would depend on where she lives. If she's living in an old people's home, then I suppose her life will be fairly regimented. Meals at certain times and organised activities and that sort of thing.

B: True. I don't think I'd like to have my life organised to that extent, but perhaps when you're her age, it's a relief not to have to deal with things like shopping and cooking. And what's more important is that she'd be living in a community. If she's living on her own, she may not be able to get out and about very much and may find herself becoming more and more isolated. That's often the case with old people.

A: Well, yes, but judging from her expression, I'd imagine that this lady isn't one of those! She could quite possibly be living with her family and helping to look after her grandchildren. I know that it's less and less the case nowadays, but it's a possibility ...

B: Mmmm. Maybe.

Stage 2 (Suggested Answer)

A: Well, I'm not an expert on advertising, but I think that the first photo would make a very effective advertisement for sunglasses. The stylish businessman has an image that many young professionals like: a tailored suit, a newspaper to keep up with the times and, of course, trendy sunglasses.

B: Yes, selling an image is a very important part of advertising. And that photograph certainly combines being fashionable with the idea of being a top professional. You know, the financial high flyer! Lots of young people aim for that image.

A: True. What about the second photo? It's closer to ordinary people, it's more realistic. So, it could be used by the government or welfare organisations to advertise assistance for families with young children. For example, day care or immunisation.

B: Yes, nowadays advertising is not only used to sell products but to help educate and inform people. More and more social welfare organisations and environmentalists are using advertising to get their message across. But on a more banal note, don't you think it could be used to advertise outdoor clothing? They are both wearing anoraks and could be setting off on some activity together. You know how advertising plays on people's emotions. All parents want to be close to their children, so the advertisers could exploit that with a caption such as 'Like father like son!'

A: Good idea! Now, obviously the third picture could be directed at young women who are interested in fashionable clothes. Or anything else related to looking good, any kind of beauty product really. You know, top model Mara Silk relies on the extra shine a certain shampoo gives her hair!

B: Or a particular brand of make-up. Now, the last picture would probably be ideal for promoting private pension funds. The old lady is happy and financially secure. Money is the last thing she has to worry about in her old age. I tend to think this would be the best one for a campaign. The elderly lady has a very expressive face, the setting is natural and I like the contrast of the bold red and yellow. I think she could persuade some of us to plan ahead. Isn't that right?

A: Well, yes it's a good photograph, but I think I'd go for the first one. If the advertisers want to sell their product, I think it presents just the image that young people would go for. And don't forget that it is the young that have the spending power these days.

B: Mmm. You're probably right. O.K. I'll go along with that. Let's agree on the first one.

Part 3

Prompt Card (a) (Suggested Answers)

Candidate A: I think that tourism has become an important part of a country's economy. In the last few decades, the tourist industry has increased hugely, mainly due to the fact that the cost of travel has decreased to such an extent that more and more people around the world are able to travel. The result is that it has become a flourishing industry which provides employment for large numbers of people, which is one reason why it's important since unemployment is always a problem. The cash tourists bring into a country also helps to boost revenues, especially in some countries where there is very little other form of income. It produces other good effects too; for example, once a country starts to develop a tourist industry, it means that certain facilities have to be provided to encourage the tourists to come, so transport and roads tend to be improved, as well as airports of course. This, in turn, leads to the provision of things like health care facilities and other services such as banking and shops. Of course, there are other benefits of tourism, too. Travel broadens people's minds, it's a very effective way to understand other cultures and have fun in the process. When people come into direct contact, they can exchange ideas or learn about the customs of that country. In that way, they may begin to understand different ways of life, and maybe then other customs don't seem so strange. Tourism can definitely help international understanding because nowhere is isolated any longer. I think that is one of its most important functions.

Candidate B: The tourist industry offers exciting jobs in hotels, restaurants or as a tour guide, in which you can meet people from all different parts of the world. If it weren't for tourism, many isolated villages or small towns wouldn't be able to survive.

Candidate A: I think tourism is necessary but it has a lot of disadvantages for locals, too.

Prompt Card (b) (Suggested Answers)

Candidate B: There are various reasons why tourists come to my country, but I think probably the main ones are history and natural beauty. My country is well known for its natural beauty, not only because of its beaches and crystal blue waters, but the landscape is so varied that people can go walking, mountaineering and canoeing, too. For example, in the winter tourists come to ski on mountain slopes and stay in traditional villages. In the spring, people are attracted by the wildlife and enjoy taking long walks through the forests of the country's national parks. We have a very rich history and there are countless historical sites, from ancient temples to medieval castles, which attract those people who are not necessarily interested in lying on a beach or taking part in a sport. So, we tend to have tourists who are interested in the culture and fascinated by the past, as well as those who simply want to relax in beautiful surroundings. It's also a country which is well known for its folklore, so there are countless traditional festivals for those who are interested in that, as well as open-air concerts and performances of various kinds. And because we are a very sociable people, there is always something going on and there is plenty for the tourists to do, they never have to feel bored!

Candidate A: Yes, it is. Tourists come from neighbouring countries because they can enjoy a cheap holiday, especially since they can camp practically anywhere. They're close to the sea and can spend time relaxing in the sun. Also, it's cheap and easy to get around, especially by train.

Candidate B: On the whole, yes. But I do think prices in some resorts can be ridiculously high.

These questions may be answered as monologues by each student individually or may develop into a discussion between both students (see answers to Test 3). (Suggested Answers)

- Mass tourism can be a problem, especially for small places. Many villages or towns lose their character since huge, ugly hotel complexes spring up everywhere to cater for large numbers of package tourists and the whole area is given over to shops, bars and restaurants only for the tourists. Then, the natural beauty of the landscape and beaches is often ruined by uncontrolled building. I think the worst thing is that, as it is today, tourism is a seasonal occupation, so people try to make a living for a whole year in just a few short months, which means that more traditional occupations, such as farming, are abandoned. Then, if something happens and for some reason there are no tourists, people have nothing to fall back on.

- Well, I suppose you could say that because hotels try to cater for the tourists' every need, they tend to provide the kind of food that tourists are used to eating, or at least a kind of bland international food. So, in a sense, I suppose that all food ends up tasting and looking much the same. But that only applies to the big hotels. The biggest effect has been fast food restaurants, but I'm not sure whether they are a result of tourism really, or whether they would have come anyway.

What is true is that tourists feel more comfortable eating food they are familiar with, and since everyone is familiar with fast food, they tend to eat it. That might be a reason for the large numbers of sandwich bars and fast food outlets we have, which of course we go to as well. So, perhaps tourism has influenced our diet a bit.

- Well, as we've said before, there are opportunities for exploiting the natural beauty of the landscape for tourism, and the countryside is ideal for some form of eco-tourism, such as walking tours in the spring and early summer or even in the winter. There's also great potential for botanists or for anyone interested in birds or wildlife, since there are many wildlife sanctuaries and protected areas to preserve certain environments such as wetlands. I think it could be a very successful way of expanding the tourist industry and deserves looking into.

- It very much depends on what a visitor is looking for, but I'd say probably a combination of natural beauty and historical interest. Most people want the place they are staying in to be attractive; nobody wants to go on holiday and look at something ugly. So, if they are going to stay in a seaside town or village, they'll want it to be picturesque, with small houses grouped around a pretty harbour, for example, rather than full of huge high rises. And they will want the natural surroundings to be unspoilt, they don't want to find themselves encircled by factories! Then, most people, however uninterested they might generally be in history, enjoy visiting some place of local interest, so that would also be a draw. So, if the people in the area want to attract visitors, they should be careful to retain the local colour!

Practice Test 2 – Paper 4 Speaking

Part 2

Stage 1 (Suggested Answer)

A: Let's start with picture 1, shall we? They're penguins aren't they?

B: Mmm, they're very sweet and obviously in their natural habitat. Look at them, I don't know if you can say birds look happy but it certainly looks to me as if they're enjoying themselves. I wonder what's making them dive into the water like that?

A: Well, at a guess, I'd say they're diving for fish ... Or, I suppose they could be trying to escape some form of predator, another animal or something like that.

B: Or a human! We're probably the biggest danger to animals living in the wild ... which brings us to picture 2. What do you think of this? It's very different isn't it, two camels and their riders, quite heavily loaded too, and what are they doing? It looks as if they are walking along the beach. It could almost have been taken from a tourist brochure.

A: Yes, in fact it probably has, but it does show something quite different from the first picture, doesn't it? These animals work for a living. They're not like the penguins who are free to do whatever they want, they are obliged to obey their masters. If they don't, they may be mistreated in some way. It's not unusual for people to regard animals that work for them as needing less care and attention than their tools do!

B: Yes, I know what you mean, but don't forget that an animal living in the wild is just as likely to suffer hardships. What if there's a spell of really bad weather? Huge numbers of animals die of starvation or are hunted for their meat or their skins. At least an animal that is used on a farm or for transport like these camels gets food and shelter. I don't think we ought to forget that.

A: Yes, it's easy to have a romantic view of animals roaming wold, isn't it? Of course, reality isn't quite like that.

Stage 2 (Suggested Answer)

A: A group wishing to promote better treatment of animals? Shall we start by talking about what sort of things we'd like to improve?

B: Right. Well, first of all there's the whole question of endangered species and the fact that due to our actions many species will soon die out! I'm sure there's something we should be promoting; a ban on hunting as a sport, for instance, or the killing of thousands of animals just to provide fur coats, which is what happens to the seals in the Arctic.

A: Don't forget about elephants. Their numbers are decreasing all the time because poachers kill them for ivory. You're right, that is certainly something we should be paying attention to. We should try to make people more aware of the fact that there are not endless numbers of animals in the world and if we go on killing them just to provide ourselves with luxuries then we shall find ourselves living in a world with no animals in it at all! The picture of the penguins conveys a sense of happiness and freedom and that could help make people see that we shouldn't destroy them. It also helps because they are such sweet-looking animals, not threatening at all.

B: That's not all, though, because the whole question links into the one of the environment. It's not just a question of our killing wild animals. We also destroy their habitats by building roads and houses or cutting down forests. We have to learn to live with them.

A: Well, we do in many cases, don't we? We have pets like the dog in picture 3! He looks like a very contented animal.

B: He certainly does, and he's a good advertisement for a well-treated animal. A lot of people don't really treat their pets very well, though I don't think it's deliberate. They just don't realise that an animal needs to live in certain conditions. A big dog shouldn't be kept locked out on a small balcony, for instance. And, of course, it needs quite a lot of food!

A: And that's just where the trouble comes in. People don't realise that the sweet little puppy they buy for their child is going to grow into a large dog with a large appetite. That's why you see so many stray dogs around. Their owners just weren't prepared for the responsibility. It's a matter of giving out proper information, really, which this photograph could help to do. You know, a happy contented pet needs ...

B: Yes, you're quite right. What about picture 4? I suppose keeping an animal as a pet is one form of captivity, while keeping it in the zoo is another.

A: Yes, though I'm not sure that in the end there's any harm in zoos. I know they get a bad press, but actually they do very good work in protecting and conserving animal species.

B: Well, there are some pretty bad zoos around where animals are kept in tiny cages with hardly any room to move, and there is no real attempt to do anything except provide a rather depressing attraction for bored children. But generally speaking, yes, I'd agree with you that zoos do quite a good job, and without them there wouldn't be so much awareness of treating animals well. Look at this tiger, you could say he was bored, I suppose, but he might just be sleepy and contented after his meal. He even looks quite friendly, he certainly doesn't look badly treated. It's not the ideal situation, obviously, but at least he's safe. I think this picture shows that animals don't have to be regarded as something we should be afraid of, that we can all coexist.

A: Yes, perhaps, which brings us back to the working animals in picture 2. It's a very attractive picture, isn't it, with the camels moving along the beach in the evening light. I think it's a very positive picture of working animals, it conveys a sense of dignity and pride, so I think it would be a good illustration of how animals should be treated. In fact, all the pictures are quite positive, aren't they? But at the

same time, even though they show animals which appear to be happy and contented, we all know that there is another side of things, so I think they would help the campaign by showing happy animals and sending out the message that this is how animals should look and behave if conditions are right.

B: Absolutely. And obviously the two most strongly contrasting pictures are 1 and 4, animals in the wild and animals in captivity, but again, getting the message across that neither situation has to be a negative one.

A: Yes, I agree with that. So we've chosen pictures 1 and 4.

Part 3

Prompt Card (a) (Suggested Answers)

Candidate A: I think social status is very important to people today, particularly because the world is changing so much, so quickly. In the past, when social levels were much more static, it didn't seem to matter so much. People had a particular status which came from their family or their job and that was more or less fixed. People knew who they were. Nowadays, you need to earn your status, it doesn't automatically come with your family or your job. New professions are becoming prestigious, like jobs in information technology or to do with the stock exchange, because they are highly paid. That's the key element today, really; social status depends on money, so everyone needs to make more and more of it so that they feel that they have some position in society. If you don't have any money, or you have a job which doesn't pay very much, then you can't expect much status. There are many people who don't let this bother them, of course, but for the majority, status has become very important, partly because of media like TV or magazines, which keep presenting us with the lifestyle that they think we should be having, or the car we should be driving and so on. We start to feel inferior if we don't have these because of the way that we link our position in society to how many things we can afford. It becomes very difficult to resist these pressures to achieve more and more and to show off what you have. It's just the old saying: keeping up with the Joneses, really, but there are many more pressures on people today to have everything, not to fall behind or be seen to be old-fashioned, to achieve and not be considered a failure.

Candidate B: Yes, I'd certainly agree that people are feeling driven to achieve nowadays. There don't seem to be so many people going in for alternative lifestyles as there were in the sixties and seventies.

Candidate A: I think people do feel as if they are pushed into conforming but I think more people rebel these days.

Prompt Card (b) (Suggested Answers)

Candidate B: I don't really think it's possible to look back to the past and say that our grandparents were happier or unhappier than our parents are today. There are many different things that can make people feel happy, anxious or sad. What is true, though, is that life now is very different in some ways, though I suppose it is still the same in many others, after all human nature doesn't really change, does it! I don't suppose that our parents are really any more materialistic or greedy than people were in my grandparent's time, it's just that there are more things at prices that most of us can afford, so I suppose we want them. I don't really think that would have been any different in the past if consumer goods had been so easily available as they are now. Of course, life in my grandparents' time moved at a much more leisurely pace. There wasn't the frantic rush to get everything done that we suffer from, or the desperate need to climb to the top of the business ladder and be the best at everything we do, so they were probably happier in the sense that they didn't suffer so much from stress. On the other hand, if they had suffered from it, they certainly wouldn't have had so many cures for it. Health care was very basic in comparison with now, which would have been very worrying, and of course education wasn't always free, or even everybody's right. So, those two aspects of life must have caused a lot of people a great deal of anxiety. In those respects, our parents probably feel much happier in their everyday lives than our grandparents did.

Candidate A: I don't know, I think people were happier in the past. Life was simpler then and there weren't so many things to worry about all the time. My grandparents lived on a farm and while they had their troubles, their life was very calm and easy compared to my parents' life.

Candidate B: I think its very difficult to judge from one generation to the other.

These questions may be answered as monologues by each student individually or may develop into a discussion between both students (see answers to Test 3). (Suggested Answers)

- That's difficult to say. I know there are many people who look back to the past and say that things were better then, but I'm not sure that there would be any advantage in returning to the past. We'd have much less stress I suppose because life would be slower, but at the same time we'd have far less time to ourselves. I have a friend who does try to reject the modern lifestyle, in fact. He won't have electricity in his house, for example. That makes everything very pretty in the evenings because he just has oil lamps, but you can't read a book or study, and to get hot water for any kind of domestic chore you have to gather wood and then chop it. Every small domestic task takes longer, and by the end of the day there isn't much time left for anything else. And you're physically exhausted. I think we probably have to look at combining what is good and practical about our modern lifestyle with what was good about the past. Try to find a way of having the labour saving conveniences we use in our daily lives but not having the stress, for instance.

- You could probably say that 'keeping up with the Joneses' is a way of keeping some people happy! Some people really enjoy it! A lot of people don't though, and it can put people under incredible strain trying to earn enough money so that they can have the same number of material things that they think everyone else has. It's something that we hear a lot about, although I'm really not convinced that everyone is busy buying smartphones and cars just because they see an advertisement on TV, and then persuading themselves that they'll be left out if they don't have them. I think the majority of people just do what people have always done, which is get on with their lives in a fairly quiet and modest way, try to provide for their families and be as happy as they can. And for most people, personal happiness isn't found in material possessions but in personal relationship or achievements. So, no, I don't think that people have sacrificed personal happiness to keeping up with the Joneses.

- I don't really know. I don't think many people know what they want from life. At least when they are very young, a lot of people just drift along from day to day and take what comes along. These people can be lucky and find that what they end up with is something that they really like, or if they're not so fortunate, they find that it's not what they want to be doing in their lives, which makes them feel frustrated and dissatisfied. But perhaps, the discovery that this is not what they want to be doing is enough to make them focus on what they do want and get out and find it, which if they look hard enough they probably will. On the other hand, I think that those people who know what they want from an early age are very lucky and actually, because they are so focused, they usually end up getting what they want out of life, maybe not exactly as they had planned it but near enough. So it depends. The trick is to decide what you want and go for it!

- I think the advantages far outweigh the disadvantages. I've always wanted to live with all my aunts and uncles and cousins close by, not necessarily in the same house, that would be a bit claustrophobic, but in the houses around. It would mean that you could always have a change of environment; your cousins would be like extra brothers and sisters and your aunts and uncles like extra parents. There would be grandparents to spoil you, too. It would also mean that individual families would not have to carry the whole burden of responsibility for dependants, as happens now. Everybody would be there to help with young children or elderly relatives who need care. There would be no need for anyone to feel lonely either, especially in the case of old people, who often feel useless and shut out. I realise, of course, that there are disadvantages, like quarrels, which are inevitable in a family, and the fact that along with increased help and companionship would go an almost complete lack of privacy and solitude, but I think that is a small price to pay for the advantages it could bring.

Practice Test 3 – Paper 4 Speaking

Part 2

Stage 1 (Suggested Answer)

A: Picture 1 looks like some sort of solar panel, doesn't it?

B: Yes, but whether it's for generating electricity from solar power or some sort of heat exchanger, it's hard to tell.

A: I think it's probably for electricity because I can't see any water tank. It's in a forest somewhere quite remote, by the look of it. Living in such a place would have been quite difficult without power.

B: Yes, I can imagine. People would have had to burn wood to provide heat and rely on candles or oil lamps at night. It would have made life much slower and more tiring.

A: Right. It's a good thing for the environment to use solar power. It's free for a start, and doesn't use up any natural resources such as wood or fossil fuels. It can also power things that are essential for communication such as telephones.

B: Absolutely. With a solar panel and a satellite dish you can talk to anyone in the world wherever you are. Can you imagine what it must have been like to be cut off and not able to communicate?

A: It must have been very difficult, I would think. Nowadays, it's almost impossible to be completely cut off from the rest of the world.

B: Unless, of course, you deliberately want to be isolated. The satellite dish in picture 3 looks like a communications antenna. I've heard that those satellites can determine somebody's exact position, anywhere in the world.

A: That's right. In the past, sailors had to rely on a compass to navigate, but with this system it's impossible to get lost!

B: The same goes for aviation too. Even with sophisticated instruments, pilots used to get lost, didn't they? Now everyone can be found! And it means we have very rapid communications which certainly wasn't possible in the past!

Stage 2 (Suggested Answer)

A: I think we should invest money in new technologies that will help to improve people's lives. Satellite communications as in picture 3 have made the world a smaller and more peaceful place. I think we should put more money into developing even more efficient communications.

B: I don't agree, I'm afraid. The private sector has more or less tied up global communication. Look at the Internet. That's almost entirely self-supporting. It's become unstoppable! I'm more inclined to think our money would be better spent on improving roads like those in picture 4. The by-pass has eased the congestion I suppose, but there is still much to be done.

A: I agree with you on that but we have already spent millions of pounds. The better the roads get, the more people use them, so it is a bottomless pit.

B: We could invest in better ways of producing power. By that I mean more sustainable sources such as solar or wind power, like that in picture 1. I think we should try to educate the public not to use fossil fuels in order to improve the environment and reduce pollution.

A: The trouble with wind farms and solar panels though, is that they take up so much space. They might not pollute the atmosphere, I agree, but they are a bit of an eyesore, aren't they? That's a kind of pollution too. I agree with you about communications, though. Private companies are investing billions of pounds every year, so there is no need for governments to intervene.

B: Well, we've looked at alternative sources of power, the road system and communications. The only area we haven't discussed yet is public health, which is the subject of picture 2. I believe that investing in research into diseases and treatment would be a far better way to spend our money.

A: You may well be right. There are lots of diseases that are making a comeback because of resistance to antibiotics. Research takes a lot of money but it's important that it continues. We need to find new drugs to combat these diseases, some of which are killers.

B: You're right, but prevention is better than cure, so I think it would be more appropriate to develop new vaccines to eradicate these diseases at source. After all, look at smallpox. It's now been officially announced that there is no more smallpox anywhere in the world. The long-term benefits of the original research have been enormous.

A: That's true, but I still think we need new drugs to combat diseases like malaria. If we were to invest in research to find a way to get rid of malaria, it would improve people's lives tremendously. If scientists had the money, they could either find a new drug or a vaccine. They might one day even use genetic engineering to stop the mosquitoes from carrying the malaria parasite.

B: Well, we don't get much malaria around here, but I see your point.

A: So, let's recap. Solar energy is largely a matter for individual investment. I don't think that tearing up even more of the countryside to make way for roads is a good idea, either, really. What do you think?

B: No, perhaps not. We agree that the communications industry have enough money from private investors and companies, so that only leaves the health issue.

A: So, we both agree then that we should invest money in medical and scientific research?

B: Yes, that's right.

Part 3

Prompt Card (a) (Suggested Answers)

Candidate A: I think the workplace will be very different in fifty years' time. Already there are many people who work from home, using their computers rather than working in an office. I think that other types of workplace will change too. People are already doing their shopping over the Internet; perhaps in fifty years there will be no need for traditional shops any more. Mundane work in factories will almost certainly disappear. The use of robotics has already revolutionised the automobile industry. In the future, I believe we will have robots that will design and build other robots. There has been a trend over the last fifty years for the working week to become shorter, and I see no reason why this trend should not continue. Fully automated factories will almost certainly give people much more leisure time. Certain occupations in the past have always been stereotyped as being suitable for one gender or the other. Nursing, for example, has been a typically female dominated profession, whereas firefighters have tended to be male. Gender roles, however, are rapidly becoming old fashioned. There are very few jobs that cannot be undertaken by either gender. People will not have to be physically strong to do any job. The use of machines will see to that, so I envisage a future where there is no distinction as to who does what. Everyone will be equal when it comes to applying for a job.

Candidate B: I think the working environment will change, but I don't think everybody will be working and shopping from home. People will always need to interact with other people, otherwise they will become isolated.

Candidate A: Some jobs are more suited to working from home than others.

Prompt Card (b) (Suggested Answers)

Candidate B: I think that most jobs are fairly paid, but there are one or two disparities. Athletes and entertainers often earn millions through their work. Who is to say that their work is more important than that of a sewage worker or a refuse collector? It could be argued that athletes and entertainers deserve their high earnings, but I don't believe they should earn so much. Nurses, for example, have always been badly paid, despite working very hard.

In some countries, particularly in the developing world, people are very poorly paid for what they do. Their gross national product may be low, which means they cannot afford to pay high salaries to their engineers or technicians. Then there is the question of jobs that require years of training. It seems unfair that a pop singer should earn so much more than someone who has had to struggle to gain professional qualifications. I think that if people take the time and trouble to study for qualifications, they should be fairly rewarded for their efforts.

I would tend to think that it is a question of degree, I don't think a refuse collector, for example, should be paid as much as a doctor, but I don't think they should be badly paid either; after all they are doing an essential job. Similarly, I think that athletes and entertainers are paid out of all proportion to their value.

Candidate A: I think athletes and entertainers deserve every penny that they earn. After all, they bring enjoyment to millions of people and that should be reflected in their earnings. Some important jobs that require a lot of qualifications should also be well paid, such as surgeons and doctors. I do think some jobs are more important than others, though.

Candidate B: I think that earning should be related to qualifications and benefit to society.

These questions may be answered as monologues by each individual student or may develop into a discussion between both students. (Suggested Answers)

- **A:** Yes, I think people should be able to go wherever they want in search of a job. It stands to reason that if there is a shortage of, say, technicians in a country, that country's government should welcome foreign labour. I think there is a danger, however, of actually causing unemployment when it involves people accepting very low wages for a particular job.

  B: People should stay in their own country when it comes to jobs. I don't believe it's possible to maintain national security with an open border policy. Lots of people come to my country claiming to be refugees, but really a lot of them are economic migrants. They contribute to unemployment by taking jobs away from our own people. I don't think people should be free to cross international borders for any reason. Far too many of them arrive with a tourist visa and then just disappear into the black economy.

- **B:** Why should the state provide employment for people who have been made redundant? Workers are redundant because their services are not longer needed. It's up to them to find another job, not the state. In any case, you can't just create jobs from nothing. There has to be a genuine need for workers.

A: People who have been made redundant expect to receive unemployment pay from the state, but in my view, they should be made to do something for the money they get. There are plenty of jobs these people could do, such as working in old people's homes or even picking up litter or keeping state-owned parks and gardens tidy.

- **A:** Yes. When people get too old to work any more, they should be entitled to a pension. In a caring society, we have to protect the weak and the infirm. A lifetime spent working should be rewarded with a pension at the end of a working life. I feel that everybody should be entitled to the same basic pension.

  B: I don't think the state should provide pension for all. Only people in genuine need should get one. In my view, people should be encouraged to set money aside for their own pensions, particularly if they are in the higher income groups.

- **B:** I don't think it's much of a threat at all. There are plenty of jobs available Look at the jobs section in any newspaper; there are hundreds of jobs advertised. People who have become unemployed only have to have the right skills and, if necessary, they could retrain for a different job.

  A: Where I come from, it's an enormous threat. It's all very well to say retrain for a different job, but that is not always practicable. Take for example someone who has become unemployed just a few years before they were due to retire. What employer would want to invest in retraining somebody for only a short-term period of employment?

Practice Test 4 – Paper 4 Speaking

Part 2

Stage 1 (Suggested Answer)

A: Well, I think the pictures are typical of the way young people of today express themselves, especially the picture showing graffiti. It portrays their frustration and boredom, and possibly their need to express their creativity.

B: Mind you, it also shows their lack of respect for other people's property. I mean graffiti isn't a means of brightening up inner-city walls any longer, as it once was. It's become a trend and young people feel they can just deface any wall or building they come across. Let's face it, there's hardly anyone's house or property that doesn't display some form of it nowadays.

A: That's true, and even the threat of being caught doing it doesn't seem to deter them.

B: I think the need to make a personal statement is clearly shown in the second picture. Young people today try their hardest not to conform to society's rules. You find they dress outlandishly, probably just to be noticed or to show their indifference to their elders.

A: Well, there's that and the possibility of rejection from their peers. I mean, when was there ever a period in time when young people didn't want to make a statement to the rest of society? If it wasn't in their choice of make-up or clothes, it was found in their music or behaviour. Personally, I like the way young people look today. They're colourful and bold and their appearance is anything but offensive. Even so, the girl in the second picture looks rather thoughtful, I think, as if she isn't truly satisfied with her lot.

B: Mmm ... I know what you mean. The picture gives you the impression that she feels trapped despite the freedom that she very likely has. She looks deep in thought, as if she's wondering what the future holds in store for her.

A: Yes. I'm sure a lot of today's youth feel the same.

Stage 2 (Suggested Answer)

A: The pictures seem to show that young people need to channel their energy into something more positive. Pictures 2 and 3 most definitely show that young people are bored, that they need something more in life to motivate them. Don't you agree?

B: Oh yes. The boys in the third picture show this quite clearly. I mean, if you have to leap off buildings to get rid of your excess energy, then that in itself shows you the need society has for more facilities and activities for young people to be involved in. Like the person in picture 4, OK, she's probably playing the kind of music that a lot of people don't approve of, but at least she has an interest in something. You know, a purpose in life.

A: Exactly. It doesn't really matter what the activity is as long as they are involved, something that makes them feel they are part of the society and not just out there on their own. Like the picture showing graffiti, for example, there's a creative instinct there that needs to be channelled.

B: And this is where the authorities come in. Schools could be doing much more than they are. They should spend more time and effort creating fulfilling activities for young people, which involve them and help them to bring out and recognise the talents they have, especially nowadays when there is so much unemployment. They are the first people to criticise young people's behaviour, yet they insist on turning a blind eye to the causes of it.

A: Yes, I must agree with you there!

Part 3

Prompt Card (a) (Suggested Answers)

Candidate A: Well, no. I don't think you can really judge a person by what they wear. Not entirely, I mean. After all, many people don't pay much attention to their appearance. As long as they're clean and reasonably tidy, then that may be enough for them. On the other hand, there are some people who are fanatical about their appearance, you know, wouldn't be seen dead without a hair out of place. Again, this doesn't mean they are that particular about everything they do. I believe the saying "first impressions go a long way" is true, though. After all, you wouldn't turn up for an interview wearing a tracksuit and trainers, would you? Society does expect us to conform to convention, and most people comply with it even if they don't agree. And then again, not everyone can afford to dress the way they might like to; this doesn't mean that they are not respectable members of society. I'm a follower of fashion myself, so I can't really criticise it too much, I suppose.

Candidate B: I'd like to say that, while I go along with what you say, I think you can make some judgements about people from what they wear. People often use dress to make some sort of statement about themselves and their beliefs. To show solidarity with a sub group they associate themselves with.

A: Actually, I don't think it's possible to be unaware of fashion. The shops stock nothing but what is in fashion every season, so it's impossible to buy something new which is not also fashionable.

Prompt Card (b) (Suggested Answers)

Candidate B: Yes, I think life in these times is a lot more demanding than it used to be. In times gone by, I think, there was less pressure on people to be perfect, you might say. As long as you were an honest upstanding member of society, you were accepted. Nowadays, many young people fear rejection from their peers if they fail to meet the standards they set. This is noticeably so in their appearance. In order not to stand out or be different from the masses, they go along with things that they would normally reject. There's too much pressure on young people to fit into certain moulds, and apart from anything else, it restricts them from showing their own individual personalities. Unfortunately, that seems to be the way of life today.

Candidate A: Yes, I think that the media has a great influence on the young people of today. Magazines and TV advertisements insist on everyone being beautiful and the need to spend every last penny you have on achieving this. Most young people are fashion victims choosing only to wear what is promoted in the media.

A: You can also see that in people from other cultures who go to live in another country. Within a very short time, they start to take on the behaviour patterns of the people they live among and start to dress like them, too. For instance, if in their own countries everyone wears bright colours but in the country they have come to live in people tend to dress in darker colours, they will soon be doing it, too.

These questions may be answered as monologues by each student individually or may develop into a discussion between both students (see answers to Test 3). (Suggested Answers)

- Both directly and indirectly. I mean, in the magazines and newspapers there are pages which are dedicated to fashion in clothes, shoes, accessories and so on. We all read these, so obviously this is a direct influence on us. If a magazine shows nothing but clothes in pale blue and white, for example, we're all going to end up thinking that these are the fashionable colours to wear. But there is another way that we are influenced, and that is through TV programmes. If you watch serials or even current affairs programmes on TV, everyone is dressed in the latest fashion. So, of course we are affected by that. In fact, in the credits at the end of the programme, there is always a list of the shops which provided the clothes.

- In general, society should not be concerned with what people wear. I think it's important that individuals feel free to express themselves without society being prejudiced against them because of their choice of clothes. Of course, there are limits, and people should not be free to dress in a way that is offensive or extremely distasteful to the rest of society. Likewise, tourists and travellers should respect the culture and sensibilities of the places which they visit. This is especially true when visiting places of worship. Whether it's a church, a mosque or a temple, it will nearly always be appropriate to make sure that you are dressed modestly, and not wear what you would on the beach or at a nightclub back home.

- There are many other areas where people follow fashion – in fact, I suppose, we do in virtually every area of our lives. Take food for example; now it's fashionable to eat exotic combinations with an eastern flavour, certainly no one would dream of serving ordinary local food to guests anymore. Or cars; in the past huge American cars were fashionable, now cars are tiny. Or architecture; just by looking around the city, you can see how different periods have different ideas about what

was attractive. It's certainly not just a question of clothes; fashion affects all aspects of our lives.

- It's difficult to ignore fashion completely because it does affect many areas of our lives, and we can't help being influenced by it to a certain extent, whether we like it or not. To me, though, people should try not to become fashion slaves. It makes them ridiculous. Fashion, of whatever kind it is, whether we're talking about clothes or furniture or even lifestyles, shouldn't be followed blindly, but should be adapted to suit each individual. If the fashion is for extremely tight clothes, it's no good wearing them if you are very overweight – they won't flatter you. Similarly, if the fashion in interior decoration is for minimalist all-white furnishings, you shouldn't follow it if you have young children who will probably spoil the look in seconds. It's just not a practical choice.

Practice Test 5 – Paper 4 Speaking

Part 2

Stage 1 (Suggested Answer)

A: Let's start with picture 1. They look very pleased with themselves. They must've just won a baseball game.

B: Yes, they are definitely happy. Look at them giving each other high fives. They must have had some kind of victory. They probably had to work very hard to get to that point, so they must be relieved that despite the difficulties they had to face, it all paid off in the end. What do you think?

A: Well, being an athlete is not as glamorous or as easy as many believe. It is certainly physically exhausting. Practising every day, travelling from city to city and, of course, playing the games themselves are all physically demanding. On top of all that, many athletes get injured and still have to play.

B: Yes, and not only is playing sports physically gruelling, it is also emotionally trying. Imagine not being with your family and friends and missing special moments or important celebrations because you're on the road. I mean, you have to sacrifice a lot if you want to win. Anyway, let's move on to picture 3 now. It is obvious they are graduating from university. They look happy and yet they also look thoughtful.

A: Don't they? It's difficult to say for sure, but they might be thinking about all that they've gone through to reach that point. Obviously, studying and attending classes requires great effort and determination.

B: That's very true. Some of the graduates might have had to support themselves, and so had to work along with attending to their studies. Having to work in order to eat and keep a roof over your head is a challenge, let alone having to pay for university tuition. It's definitely difficult trying to juggle university and work.

A: And let's not forget a social life. After all, we are human beings and we need social contact. The people in the pictures are glad they've succeeded, there's no doubt about that, but along the way they were not only physically and mentally exhausted but also emotionally exhausted.

Stage 2 (Suggested Answer)

A: Well, all of these people have achieved some sort of success and their attitudes did definitely lead to it. It goes without saying that your attitude can either lead to success or failure.

B: I agree with you on that. And you know, even if you have a positive outlook from the very beginning, each time you encounter an obstacle or even meet with failure, your attitude is tested. It can change for the worse. It's hard to focus on your goals when you're struggling.

A: Take picture A. It's highly unlikely these baseball players won every game they played. They might even have lost many consecutive games, and that can be devastating not only to the individual players but also to the whole team. When you're on a team, everybody has to constantly motivate each other and encourage each other. And that's hard to do when you yourself feel like a failure.

B: Right. And it's doubly hard to feel positive when you're in the public eye. We can't tell from the picture, but these players may be professional athletes and, as such, they are constantly criticised by the media. Not only is their playing scrutinised, but sometimes their personal life is too. An athlete's success is greatly dependent on being focused on what they do. Imagine thinking about scoring, for example, when your marriage has been on the front page of the newspaper.

A: The woman in picture 2 might be in the very same position. We don't know for sure but if we assume she is a politician, she has to get votes and maintain support from the public. Her attitude has to be exemplary. Her image is important to her success. She has to show her human side, but she must be careful, too. She can't be arrogant or show fear or defeat in any way.

B: And if she does, the people and media will lash out at her. It could mean the end of her career. And it's not easy for a woman to be in politics. It's

a field which is still dominated by males and society is still very sexist. She has to believe she can do it and look as if she can. Otherwise, she won't succeed.

A: The same goes for the woman in picture 4. Unlike the one in picture 2, this woman has entered the field of medicine. This profession is also predominantly male, and there are still many people who prefer to seek medical advice from a man than from a woman. In her practice, she probably has to face such views. Even during her academic studies she may have had to encounter such sexist attitudes. Studying medicine can be difficult enough without having to deal with negative opinions about your gender. Don't you agree?

B: Yes, and as we said before, your attitude can either make or break you. If the female doctor has succeeded, it can be attributed to her defiant attitude to various pressures and her determination to make it. If we go back to the picture we discussed before, picture 3, we can also say the same thing.

A: Yes, students have to adopt a positive attitude and maintain it, regardless of what pressures and difficulties they face. You have to keep on trying when you get a bad test mark, and keep your head when you can't get the research material you need to write the assignment due for the next day, or else it'll bring you down. You can actually perpetuate the whole situation if you don't stop yourself from giving in to negative feelings.

B: You're absolutely right. Although students have to be realistic about their weaknesses, they can't dwell on them or feel sorry for themselves because that won't help them get better. Success comes to those who are sensible and who maintain some kind of belief that they can achieve what they are striving for.

Part 3

Prompt Card (a) (Suggested Answers)

Candidate A: I think traditions still play a significant role in my culture and they can be experienced in various aspects of our everyday life, as well as in celebrations. It is very common, for example, to ask someone how they will be celebrating Easter, because it is expected that they will observe all the customs and traditions that go with it. In this way, history isn't forgotten but a living part of our daily lives. Stories are passed on from generation to generation, so that the past remains a part of who we are and influences how we view matters. In my view, traditions have a binding effect on the people observing them and, as such, give us our common identity. In this way, we keep our sense of who we are, which gives us a feeling of continuity, linking us to our ancestors. However, even though traditions play a great role in my culture, their importance and prominence is declining as we see fewer people observing holidays, or even knowing the reason why a tradition is followed.

Candidate B: I think that there is a trend back to the traditional now, people are looking for old ways of doing things, perhaps because of all the changes we are experiencing in modern life.

Candidate A: I think its only a superficial trend. Basically, a fashion.

Prompt Card (b) (Suggested Answers)

Candidate B: The world is changing so rapidly. In fact, it's difficult for us to keep pace with everything that is going on. A few years ago, only a few people had mobile phones and now we can't do without them to keep in touch with our friends. Soon, apparently, we'll be using them for all kinds of other things, too. So the spread of information has become extremely rapid. In fact, some people say that we are suffering from too much information. I think, one of the most important effects of these advances, though, has been in the workplace. Since almost all work is now computerised, there is no real need any more for heavy manual labour, which has meant that most jobs are now open to both sexes. Women can do almost everything that men used to do because there is no longer any need for great physical strength. It's also true that having more hi-tech appliances to take care of the household tasks means that families have more time to be together and more free time for leisure activities, although, perhaps, some people would say that there is too much free time and that too many parents and children spend their time on the Internet rather than socialising. So, it is perhaps true to say that due to technology, we might have become less sociable and more likely to keep ourselves to ourselves. And certainly we have become physically less active, which is why so many of us spend time at the gym!

Candidate A: I think social and family relationships have definitely benefitted from the ease of contact afforded by technological advances such as mobiles and the internet.

Candidate B: I think that's true to a certain extent but I think too many people are sacrificing their closest relationships for virtual online ones.

These questions may be answered as monologues by each student individually or may develop into a discussion between both students (see answers to Test 3). (Suggested Answers)

- I don't think it is really possible to avoid change. It doesn't matter how much we may dislike it, changes happen. Perhaps the only thing we can do is to take care that we don't accept change for its own sake, and try to make sure that we support the kind of change that is likely to lead to improvements rather than make our lives worse. One example of that would be something like cloning or genetic engineering, where most people are taking a cautious 'wait and see' approach rather than either rejecting it completely or rushing to accept it without thinking. So, on the whole, I'd say it's important not to avoid change but to accept that it has to happen.

- Well, it's true that the world is changing very rapidly and that, in many cases, traditions are becoming forgotten as technology becomes more and more important. But I feel that, perhaps, there is even more of a place for tradition now than ever before, just because the world is changing so quickly. When everything around you is constantly changing, traditional ways of doing things are very comforting, in a way, and make people feel that there are some things that are permanent and that won't change. It's like a kind of security blanket! Tradition has also become something that people are using as a way of saying that a product is of high quality. When we are faced with mass produced articles, which are often shoddy, we tend to think of something made in a traditional way as having a guarantee of quality.

- The most significant changes in recent years have probably been in communications. It's now possible, through the Internet and satellites, for all of us to know immediately what is going on in any part of the world. There's an amazing amount of information coming at us from all directions, and we are much more well-informed than previous generations were. Families and friends, for example, can now keep in daily contact wherever they are, and we are really much closer to becoming citizens of the world. This is also seen in the way that national frontiers are becoming more open and people are moving all around the world to find work. So, we are getting to know people from all countries much better. In the long run, this may help to decrease international tensions and make it more likely that we can achieve world peace.

• First of all, none of us really knows what the future will bring, so we may find that our cultural values coexist with new technological developments, for example. It's a difficult question to answer because there are so many things that make up a particular culture. I suppose that if enough people consider certain values important, then these are unlikely to change whatever the future might bring, but if these people want some things to change, then they will. I think that is the key really, the number of people who adhere to a particular way of thinking or behaving. What I mean is if, say, you decide to emigrate to a country where the culture is very different from your own, then it's going to be fairly difficult to maintain your own cultural values. After a couple of generations, it's likely that your family will have become completely assimilated into the other culture. There are a lot of people on the move at present, so there should be quite a cultural mix fairly soon.

Practice Test 6 – Paper 4 Speaking

Part 2

Stage 1 (Suggested Answer)

A: Shall we start with picture 1? He looks furious, doesn't he?

B: Yes, he does. He's probably a businessman. It seems as though he's in a hurry to reach his destination. He must be stuck in traffic, perhaps there's a hold-up of some kind. If you were in his shoes, how would you feel?

A: To tell the truth, I'd find being stuck in traffic quite annoying if I was in his position. There's nothing worse than having to wait in a queue of traffic when you're in a rush. It's very frustrating to spend so much time bumper to bumper, hardly moving.

B: But there will always be certain times of the day when the roads are more congested, because so many people leave or come home from work at roughly the same time. The rush hour is a part of everyday life for most people. I wouldn't find it so stressful because it's an unavoidable situation.

A: Yes, that's a good point, but traffic at a complete standstill is enough to drive anyone mad.

B: Yes, I suppose you're right. It's obviously a waste of time to have to wait for hours and not get anywhere, but sometimes it may be unavoidable, for example, when there's a pile-up on a dual carriageway. Perhaps that's what the policeman is doing in picture 2, calling for assistance at the scene of an accident.

A: Well, that's a job that would cause me great stress, having to deal with problems on the roads. When there has been a bad crash, policemen have to take swift action and, no doubt, see horrific sights.

B: Hmm, that's right, but a policeman's job is rewarding. It must be gratifying to know that you have saved someone's life or helped to resolve the problem of a traffic black spot.

A: Yes, I agree, but there are so many fatalities on the roads nowadays, and it's the task of the police force to regulate this. The policeman will have to take his problems home with him, and there is very little public sympathy for the police. I think I would find it very stressful to be constantly on the alert, and to have to deal with distressing and often frightening situations.

Stage 2 (Suggested Answer)

A: The effects of stress on everyday life. That's a very interesting and topical subject, isn't it? I'm sure that everyone would benefit from learning about that, whatever their level of stress is.

B: Certainly. Let's take the stress of driving all day for work. People who are out on the road, driving all day, have to face all sorts of traffic and road conditions as well as having to concentrate on their driving. In order to prevent stress levels increasing, I would say that this group of people should try really hard to relax at every available opportunity.

A: You mean, listening to relaxing music during traffic queues rather than worrying about meeting a client? That seems like sound advice. I would also add that people should try to organise their daily agenda to avoid being in areas at times when traffic reaches a peak.

B: That also applies to people who work to deadlines in offices and who constantly find themselves shouting down the phone, like the man in picture 3. Organising and prioritising workload can lead to greater efficiency and less pressure.

A: People should also make time for themselves during the day. This may involve not allowing any disturbances for one or two hours in the morning, for example. In this way, a person can get their work done much more productively and have more free time to deal with other tasks.

B: Not forgetting, of course, that this would make them more receptive to others and would relieve the pressure of mounting tasks. More generally though, people should take at least 5 minutes out of their day to take stock of their situation. The policeman in picture 2 should do that, for example. What's more, it's important to unwind after a hard day and to cleanse the mind of any stress or tension.

A: On the other hand, there are people who like to vent the frustrations of everyday life by doing something more strenuous, such as running or playing squash. This can help a person to rid themselves of all their pent-up frustrations or anger and after exercising, they will feel refreshed and more likely to have a restful night's sleep.

B: I agree with you there. Stress is a deadly killer and yet there are so many ways to avoid or control it: regular holidays, realising that there is more to life than work, that health is much more important.

A: For people who are not working, stress can also mount. Job seekers should try to take a positive approach to looking for a job. Many unemployed people feel worthless, yet if they were to realise that they possess many skills, it would help to create a positive attitude to jobs and even success in interviews. Job seekers should focus on their skills and aim at matching these skills to an appropriate job.

B: That's right. And all hope is not lost for people who feel their skills are lacking. There are many workshops and schemes that people can attend to develop skills. At the end of the day, there are many opportunities and the unemployed should try neither to set their sights too high nor too low, but instead aim for what they are best at and feel most comfortable with.

Part 3

Prompt Card (a) (Suggested Answers)

Candidate A: As far as I'm concerned, there are many influences on educational choices. Personally speaking, no person or thing had a major influence on the decisions I made. There are some children who feel obliged to follow in the footsteps of their parents, particularly if their parents are doctors or lawyers. In my case, my parents encouraged me in all subjects and helped me to develop an interest in all topics, through reading or explaining things to me. When it came to deciding which options or subjects to take at school, I was partly swayed by what my friends were interested in doing, but I also realised that my future was important and since I had always wanted to be a vet, I knew that Science and Mathematics were essential to fulfilling this ambition. I also happened to be good at Biology and Chemistry, which helped. We also had a Careers Open Day at school, which was extremely useful. I discovered that Latin would help me considerably. Parents, peers, prospects and professional people all had their part to play in shaping my education.

Candidate B: I think that our teachers have a substantial role to play in making choices about our path of education. For example, a good teacher will bring out the best in even the weakest student who may discover hidden talents. I remember a chemistry teacher of mine who really wanted me to continue studying his subject because it came so easily to me – even though at the time I had no intention of following a career that was chemistry-related. I later found it useful in my environmental studies course.

Candidate A: Yes, there's no doubt that teachers also have an important role to play in guiding students in their education choices.

Prompt Card (b) (Suggested Answers)

Candidate B: There seems to be an increasing number of parents who are opting to educate their children at home. For academic purposes, this is probably extremely beneficial to a child, since he or she will receive undivided attention for all subjects, and if there are any problems in understanding, more time can be spent explaining or clarifying misunderstandings. This, of course, depends on the teaching ability of the home tutor. In a sense, though, children learn in class from interacting with others. In certain circumstances, two heads are better than one; by this I mean that working on a group project often brings out more ideas than working alone. On this note, there is also the social aspect of home tutoring to consider; whilst school children may not develop their academic skills as quickly as home tutored ones, learning is not purely academic. Social interaction is important, home tutoring may deprive children of essential skills such as team work, which may affect their performance in the workplace. There is also the notion of friendship to consider. Being supportive of others and having a sense of belonging and not being lonely all have their part in a child's education.

Candidate A: I think that in some instances, for example in areas where school classes are overcrowded, home tutoring would have a positive effect on a child. If a child has good academic ability, being with thirty other children could have adverse effects on his or her learning and indeed be depriving him or her of a bright future.

Candidate B: I think that parents should try to incorporate as many of the subjects taught in conventional schools as possible into the home teaching course for their children. This would mean that non-academic subjects such as athletics would also need to be given attention. This would really be a further advantage for home schooling.

These questions may be answered as monologues by each student individually or may develop into a discussion between both students (see answers to Test 3). (Suggested Answers)

- I think that school facilities can always be improved in some way or another, but one area where I think most schools need to improve in is non-academic facilities. Most schools only concentrate on providing classrooms and teaching aids, and forget that children need room to run and play in order to be fresh for the next round of lessons after the breaks. So, I think that all schools need large playgrounds. Sports facilities are important for the same reason, so schools should invest in extensive playing fields facilities for a variety of sports. There should also be ample space for children to develop interests such as music and drama, too. The other important area where most schools are lacking in facilities is information technology. All schools need to be equipped with computer rooms to provide children with the tools they need in the world outside. After all, not every child is able to have these things at home.

- Schools have to take responsibility for that if it happens. There are always exceptions but in most cases, if a child fails to learn, it is because his or her interest hasn't been aroused and that is usually the fault of poor teaching. Or it could be because the lesson has been so badly taught that the child simply hasn't been able to understand and, as time has gone on, has lost interest. There are other factors too, but they also relate to the school. Classes might be so big that the teacher is unable to make sure that all children are following, or the school might be inefficiently run, with no proper substitution system for example, so that if a teacher is ill, no lesson takes place. So, yes, I'd say schools should be accountable.

- It's difficult to say which of all the available subjects children should be obliged to take, but I think, probably, their own language, a foreign language and mathematics are fairly basic and should be mandatory. Having a good command of your own language, both written and spoken, is vital and mathematics is another essential in daily life. I know because I was allowed to give up mathematics quite early on. Although I was quite pleased at the time, it was a struggle for me and I have never stopped regretting it, since mathematical calculations come into all aspects of daily life. So, I tend to think that at least mathematics should be compulsory, but with some provision made for those who are not as good at it as others.

- That's a question that is quite controversial. Ideally, schools should be offering a general education, building up a child's general knowledge and producing future citizens with a well-balanced, well-rounded view of life. But in actual fact, I don't think we can ignore the fact that the world has become very competitive. Schools have to accept that and try to prepare children to enter the world of work. I don't mean that they should stop teaching anything that is not going to lead to a career, or that children should be obliged to choose their future jobs while they are still at school, computer skills for example, or practical applications of science subjects. But schools can't pretend that the children will not soon be looking for jobs, so they must adapt to this reality.

Practice Test 1 – Paper 3 Listening

This is the Certificate of Proficiency in English Listening Test. Test 1.

I'm going to give you the instructions for this test. I'll introduce each part of the test and give you time to look at the questions.

At the start of each piece you'll hear this sound:

TONE

You'll hear each piece twice.

Remember, while you're listening, write your answers on the question paper. You'll have five minutes at the end of the test to copy your answers onto the separate answer sheet.

There will now be a pause. Please ask any questions now, because you must not speak during the test.

PAUSE 5 seconds

Part 1

Now open your question paper and look at Part One.

PAUSE 5 seconds

You will hear three different extracts. For questions 1-6, choose the answer (A, B or C) which fits best according to what you hear. There are two questions for each extract.

Extract One

PAUSE 15 seconds

TONE

Hello again ... today I'm working on a foliage garden ... probably the best solution for those of you who have one of those dark corners to fill up in a garden. Most of the plants I'm using will grow in light shade and for anyone who suffers from hay fever, it's an extra bonus as there's no pollen from blooms. You can create brilliant effects using structural plants and contrasting leaf shapes and have fun threading different variegations through them in swirls. Good leafy plants come in all shapes and sizes from big trees, bamboos and evergreens to smaller grasses and perennials, and they can be put together in loads of different ways. They lend themselves to being mingled with rocks, wood or cobbles so they are great for patios, decking or gravel gardens. They make a wonderful backdrop for flowers and keep the garden going between bursts of colour. Thinking about what foliage you want in your garden is important, yet it's the one thing most people neglect.

PAUSE 5 seconds

TONE

REPEAT Extract One

PAUSE 2 seconds

Extract Two

PAUSE 15 seconds

TONE

Man: The opportunity to create our dream house arose when we were able to buy the farmhouse, a cottage and outbuildings along with 17 acres of land for the sum of £112,000. The house itself wasn't grand, but it had potential.

Woman: Yes, the farmhouse was structurally sound but it had been extended unsympathetically.

Man: Yeah, it had been rebuilt in Victorian times, and the internal layout was just all wrong.

Woman: There was a long corridor running through it with small rooms leading off. The ceilings were low, and the whole place was dark and pokey; it just didn't seem to have a heart.

Man: I eventually found a solution to that by completely remodelling the interior ...

Woman: So the house is now open-plan, with access to the upstairs by a staircase we built ourselves.

Man: We also incorporated a lot of reclaimed timber. The entire kitchen is built from recycled wood. It's eco-friendly and it gives the interior a mature appearance, too.

Woman: Some of the wood we used for the doors came from the cowshed and this had a particularly smooth finish. I suppose it's the result of hundreds of years of cows' tongues licking it ... *(laughter ... fade)*

PAUSE 5 seconds

TONE

REPEAT Extract Two

PAUSE 2 seconds

Extract Three

PAUSE 15 seconds

TONE

I had a friend who worked for a TV station and when I was visiting her one day, she mentioned how difficult it was to get the details right for period dramas and things like that. I mean, you can't have a serialization of a nineteenth century novel, for example, and when the hero wants to write something down, he pulls out a ballpoint pen! Well, looking for interesting odds and ends has always been a bit of a hobby of mine and so I offered to help her out. It went from there really. Initially, I started working on a freelance basis for one television channel, really to supplement the full-time job I had at that time, but I had so much work offered to me by others too, and I set up my own company in the end, and really it's proved very lucrative, as well as interesting. I'm one of those fortunate people whose hobby has turned into their job!

PAUSE 5 seconds

TONE

REPEAT Extract Three

PAUSE 2 seconds

That's the end of Part One.

Now turn to Part Two.

PAUSE 5 seconds

Part 2

You will hear a report on how English has become a global language. For questions 7-15, complete the sentences with a word or short phrase.

You now have forty-five seconds in which to look at Part Two.

PAUSE 45 seconds

TONE

Right now, English is either the dominant or official language in over 60 countries of the world. It is without any doubt a world language now, but this wasn't always the case. How did English achieve this extraordinarily wide representation? Well, English started to move around the world with the early voyages of discovery to the Americas, Asia and the Antipodes, and continued in the 19th century when colonies were established in Africa and the South Pacific. Then in the 19th century, it took a significant further step when many newly independent states adopted it as an official or semi-official language. Two factors make English important today; the expansion of British colonial power, which peaked towards the end of the 20th century, and the emergence of the US as the dominant economic power of the 20th century. It is this which continues to explain the position of the English language today – although there are people in Britain who find this difficult to accept! But if you look at the statistics, you'll see that the USA contains nearly four times as many English mother-tongue speakers in the world; this dominance gives the Americans a controlling interest in the way the language is likely to develop.

But, as we've already seen, Britain and the US are not the only places where English is used as an important vehicle for communication. In countries where English is a second or foreign language, or where English is used simultaneously as a first and a second language like Canada for example, or in a country like India, where a history of language contact has produced a legacy of language conflict, it is not easy to determine how and in what situations English is used.

One reason you find people often put forward for English having achieved its worldwide status is its intrinsic linguistic features. People have claimed that it is inherently a more logical or beautiful language than others, or it's easier to pronounce or it's simpler, or it has a larger vocabulary. This is simply not true. There are no objective standards of logic or beauty to compare different languages, and questions of phonetic, grammatical, or lexical complexity are never capable of simple answers. For example, English may not have many inflectional endings, (which is what most people are thinking of when they talk about English as grammatically simple), but it has a highly complex syntax. The number of endings actually has no bearing on whether a language becomes used worldwide. You just have to look at the success of Latin or Ancient Greek in the past to see that. There has always been one language in a particular era which was high in world esteem and probably always will. What gives a language this particular position is dependent on many factors – political, economic, social, religious, literary even, but not necessarily linguistic.

PAUSE 10 seconds

Now you'll hear Part Two again.

TONE

REPEAT Part Two

PAUSE 5 seconds

That's the end of Part Two.

Now turn to Part Three.

PAUSE 5 seconds

Part 3

You will hear an interview with Maria Stefanovich, co-founder of a creativity group which organises workshops for executives. For questions 16-20, choose the answer (A, B, C or D) which best fits what you hear.

You now have one minute in which to look at Part Three.

PAUSE 1 minute

TONE

Interviewer: Not long ago stressed out executives at embattled Marks & Spencer's were packed off on a training course. There's nothing unusual in that. But the team was in for a surprise. This was not a time management seminar, with flashy flip-charts. Instead they were faced with cardboard, paint and glue. With us here is Maria Stefanovich, co-founder of Droll, the creativity group which ran the creative workshop for those executives. What exactly did the team do with these art supplies?

Maria: During this particular day-long session, each delegate was required to create a mask to show the face they presented at work. You see, mask-making is a very effective corporate tool. Often people create faces that are anxious and alienated. The process of looking inwards and transforming difficult issues helps them access their intuitive, imaginative skills.

Interviewer: Why do you believe such an unconventional approach to seminars has caught on?

Maria: Creativity has become a prized commodity, even in such professions as accountancy. Whereas once we could drag ourselves into work, safe in the expectation of doing nothing more taxing than, er, work, now bosses have other ideas. They have begun to see that if you sit in a boring meeting in a boring conference room, you will emerge with boring ideas. All companies are hungry for new ideas, but if you push and pull in a pressured atmosphere, there's creative bankruptcy. As companies become desperate to harness creativity and lateral thinking, they are being forced to look at new ways of fostering those talents.

Interviewer: Where did such programmes originate from?

Maria: The roots of the play industry lie on the other side of the Atlantic. Ten years ago, the marketing firm, Play, pioneered the techniques now taking off here in Britain. Staff at Play invent their own superheroes and costumes. They have an office playroom and a company dog which is picked up for work even when its owner is away, and there are no conventional job titles. Instead, employees have business cards printed with peculiar slogans such as 'What if?' and 'Voice of reason'. When you turn work into a place that encourages people to be themselves, have fun and take risks, you unleash their creativity. It all comes down to employers having at last realised that a happy team is a creative one. Funnily enough, excuse the pun, most of the companies that sign up are the ones that have least need for it; young, gung-ho firms in new media and advertising. They do a lot of presentations, but their workers do them in a linear way. Creativity programmes make them think laterally. Some companies send people on adventure excursions. Creativity groups are another way of getting people focused and excited.

Interviewer: The Humberside Training and Enterprise Council found that storytelling workshops breed confidence. How so?

Maria: Storytelling workshops are particularly beneficial in confidence building. There was one woman who presented a story about how nervous she felt giving a presentation to the board. She said she felt like a rabbit caught in the headlights and her teeth felt too big for her mouth. So, we acted out a story with her as a rabbit. The humour of it allowed her to overcome that fear. These days, we are seeing everything from mime, circus skills and comedy to finger-painting. It all sounds worryingly New Age, but our company has been called in by such conservative and long-established corporations such as Smith-Kline Beecham, Hedron, Chesterton Property and government agencies. It has also worked with staff at the Industrial Society. We asked them to describe the society as if it were a landscape. At first, everyone talked about how it was a beautiful, serene place. Then someone described a bog, another a volcano about to erupt. It's all about encouraging better communication. The benefits are tangible. We've had lots of feedback about how staff bring more passion and ideas to their work. They take more risks and are more honest.

PAUSE 10 seconds

Now you'll hear Part Three again.

TONE

REPEAT Part Three

PAUSE 5 seconds

That's the end of Part Three.

Now turn to Part Four.

PAUSE 5 seconds

Part 4

Part Four consists of two tasks.

You will hear five short extracts in which different people are talking about how they travel.

Look at Task 1. For questions 21-25, choose from the list (A-H) how each speaker prefers to travel.

Now look at Task 2. For questions 26-30, choose from the list (A-H) what each speaker says about the advantages of the way they travel.

While you listen you must complete both tasks.

You now have forty-five seconds in which to look at Part Four.

PAUSE 45 seconds

TONE

Speaker 1

PAUSE 2 seconds

Whenever I have to travel, whether for business or pleasure, I prefer to travel light. Even when going on a relatively long trip, I only take a small bag with essentials. I find that not having to lug around heavy suitcases makes for a much better travelling experience. It's also great to only have hand luggage when on the plane, so there's no waiting around for baggage when I arrive. I'm just straight out once I get to my destination. And if I really think I need something while I'm away, then I can buy it when I get there. It's such a fuss free way to travel and really reduces the stress and fatigue of getting from A to B.

PAUSE 3 seconds

Speaker 2

PAUSE 2 seconds

I'm not particularly keen on travelling. I generally stay at home and potter about the garden when on holiday and I've never been abroad. I do occasionally go and visit friends and relatives for a few days and I rather enjoy the odd day trip here and there. Cars make me nauseous and buses are uncomfortable, so if I'm going anywhere, it is by train. Travelling first class is very comfortable. I can pop to London to visit a museum, meet a friend for lunch or take a trip to Brighton for some good sea air. That's a pleasant way to travel. Galavanting off across the skies is a hideous nightmare.

PAUSE 3 seconds

Speaker 3

PAUSE 2 seconds

Like many high level business executives, I travel the world for work. It's stressful but it's simply part of my job. I'm often required to go to Asia or the Americas at short notice to negotiate a deal, so, I've collected a lot of airmiles. Consequently, when I do get the chance to have a holiday, I like more leisurely forms of travel. I've been on a few cruises and I took the wife on the Orient Express last year. This year we're thinking of taking a horse-drawn caravan round Ireland. For me high speed travel and jet lag is part of a day's work. Holiday travel is about taking the time to watch the world go by.

PAUSE 3 seconds

Speaker 4

PAUSE 2 seconds

I can't think of anything worse than going on a typical tourist holiday where everything is organised and you're stuck in some plastic commercial resort with hundreds of your fellow countrymen. When I travel, I want to at least try to get under the skin of the place I'm visiting. For me, backpacking is the best way to achieve this. I try to get a month a year when I really get a chance to explore a country or region. It might mean the travelling is uncomfortable, like using crowded local buses to get around and I stay in some pretty basic rooms sometimes, but I think I do actually learn about the place I'm visiting and I get to see things no ordinary tourist would.

PAUSE 3 seconds

Speaker 5

PAUSE 2 seconds

I first started travelling with my motorbike, both at home and abroad, over 20 years ago. It's a wonderful way to get around because I can go anywhere at all and it gives me a real sense of freedom. A lot of people believe that it must be quite dangerous, especially abroad and in countries known for dangerous driving, but I've had very few spills over the years and none were that serious. But I am rather cautious when driving in unknown territories, and I do have the full complement of safety gear. Another misconception is that I have to travel with little more than a toothbrush and clean underwear. Not true! You'd be surprised how much stuff I can fit into the bike panniers.

PAUSE 10 seconds

Now you'll hear Part Four again.

TONE

REPEAT Part Four

PAUSE 5 seconds

That's the end of Part Four.

There'll now be a pause of five minutes for you to copy your answers onto the separate answer sheet. Be sure to follow the numbering of all the questions. I'll remind you when there is one minute left, so that you're sure to finish in time.

PAUSE 4 minutes

You have one more minute left.

PAUSE 1 minute

That's the end of the test. Please stop now. Your supervisor will now collect all the question papers and answer sheets.

Practice Test 2 — Paper 3 Listening

This is the Certificate of Proficiency in English Listening Test. Test 2.

I'm going to give you the instructions for this test. I'll introduce each part of the test and give you time to look at the questions.

At the start of each piece you'll hear this sound:

TONE

You'll hear each piece twice.

Remember, while you're listening, write your answers on the question paper. You'll have five minutes at the end of the test to copy your answers onto the separate answer sheet.

There will now be a pause. Please ask any questions now, because you must not speak during the test.

PAUSE 5 seconds

Part 1

Now open your question paper and look at Part One.

PAUSE 5 seconds

You will hear three different extracts. For questions 1-6, choose the answer (A, B or C) which fits best according to what you hear. There are two questions for each extract.

Extract One

PAUSE 15 seconds

TONE

Man: Soon after my parents were demobilised from the armed forces, they were lucky enough to be allocated a council house on one of the new estates that were springing up in the early fifties.
Our house was in Essex and I look back with fond memories of a happy childhood there. As a pre-teenager I used to spend the summer holidays working on the farms surrounding our estate. A short walk and I'd be listening to the rustic Essex accents of the farm workers, instead of the estuary English of the estate. Adventure playgrounds were unknown then; homes and schools were a top priority, so we devised our own adventures. Nearby was an old abandoned army camp. That become our battleground where we re-enacted the conflicts we'd heard our parents speak about. The local gravel pit became our swimming pool. Nearby quarries, where chalk had been extracted for the cement works, had left a series of tunnels, which became our 'caves' and we spent hours exploring them. Nobody had thought

of vandalism then; we were far too busy doing other things!

PAUSE 5 seconds

TONE

REPEAT Extract One

PAUSE 2 seconds

Extract Two

PAUSE 15 seconds

TONE

Man: If birds won't let you approach them, get them to come to you by setting up your own feeding station. Birds rely heavily on the food and water we provide, especially in winter. The key to success is to provide a good selection of food, which will attract a wide range of species. Depending on where you live, you may get unusual visitors such as nut hatches, woodpeckers and even the exotic ringnecked parakeet. The best way to observe a wide range of species is to find a place you can visit on a regular basis. Explore the area within a couple of kilometres of your home and look for a self-contained habitat with a good range of resident species and the potential to attract passing migrants. Visit as often as you can and keep detailed records of your observations. You'll gain a real insight into the behaviour and habits of your local birds.

PAUSE 5 seconds

TONE

REPEAT Extract Two

PAUSE 2 seconds

Extract Three

PAUSE 15 seconds

TONE

Reporter: Fears are growing for the safety of horses and riders at today's Olympic show-jumping final.
Torrential rain has turned the course into a morass, days after the disastrous start to the competition, when two horses fell and no horse was able to gain a clear round inside the time. Following more heavy rain, the riders were skating around the arena on Tuesday.
Diane Rawlins, Britain's dressage coach, stated that drainage was a problem there, with surface water everywhere. Britain's Geoff Billington, riding Otto, attacked the state of the ground, saying that for an Olympic surface it was disgusting. Team-mate Michael Whitaker says that he will be putting studs in his horse's shoes.
Show organisers blame Olympic officials for banning the use of rubber, PVC or gel when laying the arena.

Britain's Kirsty Mepham, who rides Dikkilou, said that at first she thought he would cope, but he lost confidence. She feels that this has meant their worst performance for some time.

PAUSE 5 seconds

TONE

REPEAT Extract Three

PAUSE 2 seconds

That's the end of Part One.

Now turn to Part Two.

PAUSE 5 seconds

Part 2

You will hear a radio programme about a family who gave up their suburban lifestyle for a life in the country. For questions 7-15, complete the sentences with a word or short phrase.

You now have forty-five seconds in which to look at Part Two.

PAUSE 45 seconds

TONE

Interviewer: Good morning Evan, and welcome to the programme. Now, I'm sure everyone listening today envies the kind of lifestyle you have, but they probably feel that it's just too much of a risk. Tell us what made you opt for it and what advice you would give to those who may be contemplating it.

Evan: Well, in 1998, I found myself facing mounting job insecurity and decided to take voluntary redundancy, before I was pushed, you might say. I was a further education ecology lecturer and my wife Nina an office manager, living in suburban Guildford when we decided to move to the country. Using my redundancy money to pay off our existing mortgage we used what was left to buy our smallholding in Cornwall.

It's a moderate-sized bungalow on a considerably larger piece of land, tucked into a shallow depression in the hillside, overlooking a spectacular sweep of valley. If it's a clear day, you see 24 miles to St. Austell from the lounge window. The nearest village to us is Lanner, which has a school, a church and one shop. It's two and a half miles from us, so you can see we're pretty isolated.

Our aims and ambitions are to first become as self-sufficient as possible in food and then to grow for local sale. I realise both of these things take time, and because our joint annual income has plummeted to £10,000, we are both seeking part-time employment until our smallholding begins to pay its way, which actually could take several years.

In the meantime, there's more than enough work to keep us busy. At the moment, I'm building fences to stop our experimental herd of six sheep getting into the neighbour's fields and building irrigation channels for the orchard we hope to plant. Nina is using knowledge she gained from a crash course in market gardening and protected cropping techniques to prepare the ground for an extensive garden. All back-breaking stuff! You see, although we want to end up as independent as possible, we don't want to be like some people who try to live outside society. We want to contribute, it's just that we've moved away from the traditional career ladder towards seeing what kind of simpler, greener life we can achieve in a rural community. We're not the only people who have opted for this way of life, we've simply joined the bank of disillusioned professionals who have left the insecurity of work to "downshift". We do feel that we are better prepared than most for life in the slow lane because we've always shared a strong streak of independence by shunning cars and only buying a TV set for Catriona, our daughter's sake. In Guilford, we also grew our own vegetables.

I suppose it's been the biggest gamble of our lives, but it doesn't feel like that although there are compromises. Our biggest has been to buy a car, which we swore we'd never do, but it's just too dangerous for our daughter to cycle to school down narrow country lanes, especially in winter. I try to combine the school run with other chores and we make our own entertainment and spend little. Although we don't grow much food yet, we already lead a more sustainable lifestyle, and leave less of a mark on the planet, which is hugely satisfying.

My advice to other would-be 'downshifters' would be not to expect miracles overnight. It can be quite isolating, so you have to be very resilient. You may miss the theatre, the cinema and even the buzz of city life, but the rewards are enormous. This way of life is a valuable contribution towards a more equitable, balanced society.

PAUSE 10 seconds

Now you'll hear Part Two again.

TONE

REPEAT Part Two

PAUSE 5 seconds

That's the end of Part Two.

Now turn to Part Three.

PAUSE 5 seconds

Part 3

You will hear an interview with Haile Gerselassie who has won two Olympic gold medals. For questions 16-20, choose the answer (A, B, C or D) which best fits what you hear.

You now have one minute in which to look at Part Three.

PAUSE 1 minute

TONE

Interviewer: Ethiopia has a vibrant, resilient side that does its best to help itself despite the odds. Of course, this more positive, less dramatic side of Ethiopia doesn't tend to make news headlines. With one exception, and his name is Haile Gebrselassie.

Haile Gebrselassie is regarded as one of the world's greatest distance runners. He has set 15 world records and at the Sydney Olympics he retained the Olympic Gold medal he first won in 1996 for the 10,000m, with a breathtaking, last minute spurt of energy. Haile, you're the latest in a long line of talented runners to come out of Ethiopia, what is it that gives Ethiopians an edge when it comes to running?

Haile: It's not just Ethiopia. Athletes from other Rift Valley countries also seem to have an advantage. The most likely explanation is that we live and train at high altitudes. I've been told that having been born in the mountains means that our bodies have already compensated for the lack of oxygen by having bigger lungs and more red blood cells. More blood cells seem to work more efficiently, as they make better use of oxygen and glucose is burned up faster. The overall result, I suppose, is a much-improved circulation.

Interviewer: Couldn't other athletes just train in the mountains until they've acclimatised?

Haile: Other runners have tried in the past, but it isn't as simple as that. Runners who weren't born and raised in the mountains often experience altitude problems such as vomiting and giddiness, when they return to sea level.

Interviewer: Well that explains your incredible aerobic ability, but what can you tell us about your running style, which has been described as, well, peculiar? No offence meant.

Haile: None taken, I've heard that said too often to take offence. My speciality is in the 10 kilometre events and there is a good reason for that. Every day, I used to run to and from school in Asela - a distance of 10 kilometres. Even now, I still run as if I were carrying my homework, with one arm raised slightly higher and closer to my body than the other.

Interviewer: Asela has become a sort of breeding ground for long-distance runners hasn't it?

Haile: It's probably a question of circumstances as well as altitude. Other children have video games and computers, televisions and stereo systems. They have parents with two or three cars, who will drive them to school, to the movies or to their friends' houses. Where I was born we ran. We ran because we loved the sensation of running – which was fortunate, as we also ran because we had no choice.

Interviewer: Obviously, it worked for you. Tell me about the Global Adidas running club in Addis Ababa.

Haile: We set this up. My equipment sponsor and I wanted to plough some money back into the sport. We recruit between 70 and 80 young men and women who are regarded as the best athletes in Ethiopia. The best of these get a monthly allowance. Now, there are runners everywhere in the hills. As I go for my morning run, I see 50 running along the road, when before there would be only a few. We bring the best here from my home region of Asela; it's much easier to co-ordinate the training here in Addis Ababa. We are also planning a training camp at a higher altitude, in the hills above Addis.

Interviewer: If you come from an Ethiopian highland region and prove to be the best in your school, then go on to beat all the others in your region, you're in for a shot at being the best in Ethiopia. And chances are, as the athletic records show, that would make you the best in the world. Thank you Haile.

PAUSE 10 seconds

Now you'll hear Part Three again.

TONE

REPEAT Part Three

PAUSE 5 seconds

That's the end of Part Three.

Now turn to Part Four.

PAUSE 5 seconds

Part 4

Look at Task 1. For questions 21-25, choose from the list (A-H) how each speaker got started as a performer.

Now look at Task 2. For questions 26-30, choose from the list (A-H) what each speaker says they like about their profession.

While you listen you must complete both tasks.

You now have forty-five seconds in which to look at Part Four.

PAUSE 45 seconds

TONE

Speaker 1

PAUSE 2 seconds

I started taking ballet lessons at the age of five and by the time I was 12, I was just fed up with it and wanted to give it up. I was going through puberty and in a pre-teen rebellious phase. So my parents decided to take me to Russia to go to one of the top schools there and, basically, I fell in love with dance all over again. The training is long and hard and dancers only have a few short years to make a mark on the world of dance. But nothing beats the fulfillment of doing something so beautiful, so creative. My days at work usually last about 10 hours, starting with early morning class, then some choreography and rehearsal. I usually get some massage and physio in the afternoon and then a bit of rest before the evening performance. Most people think it sounds like a terrible life but I think myself blessed.

PAUSE 3 seconds

Speaker 2

PAUSE 2 seconds

I trained as a classical musician and played double bass in a symphony orchestra for a couple of years, too. But I found working in the orchestra very rigid and stultifying. Then, friends and I formed a jazz quartet. We thought it would give us more of a chance to express ourselves musically. I lead a very peripatetic lifestyle as we play at jazz clubs and festivals all over the world. My wife is very relieved that this winter we're playing in just one London club and she'll actually get to see me. From the outside my life might seem very glamourous, travelling the world, but it can be a bit of a slog at times. Every profession has its hazards I suppose.

PAUSE 3 seconds

Speaker 3

PAUSE 2 seconds

My mother was utterly horrified that I wanted to audition for drama school and threatened to cut me off. Fortunately Daddy thought it very brave and honest of me and has always rooted for me. I got work almost as soon as I finished drama school and I've never been out of work since. Most of my jobs are stage work in rep, with a few television roles and adverts thrown in. I've never had to work as a waitress to make ends meet like many have to and although it hasn't made me fabulously wealthy or famous, I've done pretty well for myself. I would quite like to branch out into some film work, but I'm not remotely interested in Hollywood or trying to get any kind of celebrity status, much to my agent's chagrin.

PAUSE 3 seconds

Speaker 4

PAUSE 2 seconds

I first started DJing as a hobby in my teens. I love music and getting crowds up and buzzing. There's a real art to it. Eventually, I was making more money from my hobby than I was from the day job so I packed it in and went pro DJ. I would rate myself in the top 10 to 20 in the world. I do gigs all over the world. I could be doing a season in Goa, a few nights in Mykonos or a guest slot in Ibiza. The good thing is, that I can take lots of time off between gigs because the level of remuneration is very high. I'm like one of those fashion models that won't get out of bed for less than ten grand.

PAUSE 3 seconds

Speaker 5

PAUSE 2 seconds

In the past, circus performers were seen as being on the margins of society and it wasn't regarded as respectable at all. That has changed drastically in the last twenty odd years. Now there are lots of great schools teaching traditional circus skills and most circuses are about human skills and not the exploitation of animals. I applied to join the circus after leaving school at 16 and got on-the-job training, working my way up to being a full blown acrobat. The circus travels the country every summer, appearing at fairs and festivals. We have a great show that incorporates traditional circus skills with modern music and dance. It's very popular and I love being part of the performance and the fact that we have done so much to help change the image of the circus in the public's mind.

PAUSE 10 seconds

Now you'll hear Part Four again.

TONE

REPEAT Part Four

PAUSE 5 seconds

That's the end of Part Four.

There'll now be a pause of five minutes for you to copy your answers onto the separate answer sheet. Be sure to follow the numbering of all the questions. I'll remind you when there is one minute left, so that you're sure to finish in time.

PAUSE 4 minutes

You have one more minute left.

PAUSE 1 minute

That's the end of the test. Please stop now. Your supervisor will now collect all the question papers and answer sheets.

Practice Test 3 — Paper 3 Listening

This is the Certificate of Proficiency in English Listening Test. Test 3.

I'm going to give you the instructions for this test. I'll introduce each part of the test and give you time to look at the questions.

At the start of each piece you'll hear this sound:

TONE

You'll hear each piece twice.

Remember, while you're listening, write your answers on the question paper. You'll have five minutes at the end of the test to copy your answers onto the separate answer sheet.

There will now be a pause. Please ask any questions now, because you must not speak during the test.

PAUSE 5 seconds

Part 1

Now open your question paper and look at Part One.

PAUSE 5 seconds

You will hear three different extracts. For questions 1-6, choose the answer (A, B or C) which fits best according to what you hear. There are two questions for each extract.

Extract One

PAUSE 15 seconds

TONE

Woman: Now, George, calm down. I know you always had high hopes for Rob, but that doesn't mean he has to follow in your footsteps. Haven't you always emphasised, and quite rightly, that he needs to be independent? What's wrong with being a professional musician anyway?

Man: Is that what you'd call someone playing in a rock band? He looks down his nose at me and my colleagues but imagine where we'd all be now if I hadn't knuckled down and worked hard. Where does he think the money for the music lessons came from in the first place?

Woman: Oh George, don't be so pompous!

Man: Pomposity has absolutely nothing to do with it. These days, you need credible qualifications to succeed in life.

Woman: Well, George, there are a great number of very well-known people who have none ...

Man: What does a seventeen-year-old know about life? I'm sorry but ...

Woman: Would you please stop this and get back to the subject! Rob has made up his mind and I think the least we can do is to back him in his choice. After all, he is a mature, well-balanced individual who doesn't act on impulse. I'm sure it was a well thought-out decision.

PAUSE 5 seconds

TONE

REPEAT Extract One

PAUSE 2 seconds

Extract Two

PAUSE 15 seconds

TONE

Speaker: Total colour blindness, in which all hues are perceived as variations of grey, is known as achromatopsia or monochromatism. This is a far more serious defect than partial colour blindness and fortunately, extremely rare. Unlike simple colour blindness, monochromatism affects men and women equally. Partial colour blindness, called dichromatism, consists generally of the inability to differentiate between the reds and greens of the colour spectrum, or to actually be unable to perceive reds or greens. Dichromatism is the most common form of colour blindness, affecting about 7 per cent of men and less than 1 per cent of women, and is normally a hereditary characteristic. It is interesting that the vision of most colour-blind people is normal in all other respects. They can generally learn by experience to associate colours with varying sensations of brightness. Consequently, many people live their lives without even being aware that they are colour-blind! Some only discover that they have the condition when they take obligatory tests like obtaining driving licenses or when applying for certain jobs in which colour distinction is necessary.

PAUSE 5 seconds

TONE

REPEAT Extract Two

PAUSE 2 seconds

Extract Three

PAUSE 15 seconds

TONE

Speaker: If I could continue please ... As the 19th century progressed, more and more farmers who relied on the adverse terms of credit advanced by money lenders, were reduced to bankruptcy and many were ultimately forced to sell their land. The power of large land owners and merchants then drove or kept many individuals from ownership of land. By the 1840s, thousands of landless people were forced into dependent employment as farm labourers or workers on the construction of roads, canals and railways. The fact that many individuals were unsuccessful in the pursuit of employment is shown by the high rate of migration within the country and by emigration to other countries. In their new countries, despite the fact that the lives of so many people at this time had been affected by capitalist institutions, priorities of work and life were not ordered strictly in terms of economic criteria. Cultural factors were important. Upper Canadians, for example, who mainly came from the British Isles, had been exposed in their native lands to the protestant ethic and its positive enjoinment of hard work and frugality. Thus, considerations of what was useful, rather than what could be exchanged on the market, were also important in the production of goods.

PAUSE 5 seconds

TONE

REPEAT Extract Three

PAUSE 2 seconds

That's the end of Part One.

Now turn to Part Two.

PAUSE 5 seconds

Part 2

You will hear a radio report about sharks. For questions 7-15, complete the sentences with a word or short phrase.

PAUSE 45 seconds

TONE

Presenter: Few people have seen a shark breach. But in South Africa, where it is generally known as the 'blue pointer', its breaching, or leaping high out of the water, is well known enough for local fishermen to call it the 'grasshopper shark'. However, it's quite rare to see a breaching – and even rarer to capture it on film. Ralf Kiefer has done just that and spent hours waiting in a cramped boat off Seal Island in False Bay, South Africa. Ralf, why Seal Island?

Ralf: Well, Seal Island is home to 64,000 South African fur seals – the Great White's favourite wintertime prey. The depth of the water around the island gives the shark enough space for a vertical rush upwards at the seals on the surface. Elsewhere, where the water is shallow, Great Whites typically catch seals in a horizontal rush.

The key to a successful shark attack is the element of surprise. If the chosen prey becomes aware of the shark's presence and turns to face it, the shark will not usually attempt the attack. Seals have very sharp teeth and sharks are very protective of their eyes! So the Whites may use the breaching technique as a method of surprising the seal.

I waited for some hours using a dummy seal as bait to try and trick a shark into attacking it. I was about to give up when a magnificent female Great White suddenly burst out of the water at a 45 degree angle, uncovering her body's full length in less than a second, before flipping over – this happens because their weight is concentrated around their heads – and plunging back into the sea. I could even see the five rows of razor sharp teeth. Well, the dummy seal was destroyed, but I got the pictures!

Sharks are strange creatures, you know. They evolved 200 million years before the dinosaurs and their highly sophisticated template has remained virtually unchanged for the past 70 million years.

They are all very vulnerable to exploitation, though, and a few species are critically endangered in some parts of the world. Some have declined by 90 per cent over the last few years as they've become the most valuable product in the ocean. One fin from a shark can earn £15,000. And finning is big business, especially in the Far Eastern markets, where shark fin soup is an expensive delicacy reserved for special occasions. Shark meat has little commercial value, though, so once the fin has been taken the shark is thrown overboard rather than kept for food.

You see, sharks have never evolved a defence against that sort of systematic slaughter. It takes many species 15-20 years to reach reproductive maturity. Even then, a female shark will not produce great shoals of offspring. They breed only every two years and each female gives birth to just four to six pups at a time, nowhere near enough for the population to recover from the butchery it faces.

If we are going to save these extraordinary creatures, a massive change in attitude towards them is needed. They are not brutal monsters to be feared, but vulnerable fish that have swum the world's oceans for millions of years and are now in desperate need of protection.

PAUSE 10 seconds

Now you'll hear Part Two again.

TONE

REPEAT Part Two

PAUSE 5 seconds

That's the end of Part Two.

Now turn to Part Three.

PAUSE 5 seconds

Part 3

You will hear an interview with Marion D'Souza about homes exchanged for holidays. For questions 16-20, choose the answer (A, B, C or D) which best fits what you hear.

You now have one minute in which to look at Part Three.

PAUSE 1 minute

TONE

Presenter: Our guest today is Marion D'Souza who works for a company that specialises in arranging house swaps, called strangely enough, 'Houseswaps UK'. Marion, welcome.

Marion: Thank you, I'm happy to be here.

Presenter: Now Marion, when we talk of home exchanges, it's hard to imagine allowing complete strangers to take over your home for a couple of weeks. Isn't it a bit risky?

Marion: That's precisely why agencies like ours have come into being. In order to get a good match, we ask potential clients to fill in a form to obtain a myriad of details; dates available, type of home, location, number of rooms and other personal details. We also require details of the owner's profession, their families and where they would prefer to go for their holiday. That way we try to ensure that people have suitable accommodation for their holidays.

Presenter: Does any money change hands?

Marion: Not between clients, but of course we have to recoup the cost of maintaining our database and the cost of producing the catalogues. These come out every four months and we charge £50.00 per copy.

Presenter: Isn't that a bit expensive?

Marion: Not really when you consider we also indemnify against any damage to homes and that's included in the cost. People are happy to pay for their peace of mind. You have to remember that we are a growing business and like any other business, we have to make a profit in order to survive and expand.

Presenter: What sort of people are attracted by the idea?

Marion: At present, it seems to be very popular with professional, middle class people, particularly the teaching profession and the world of education generally, but as it catches on, I would expect to see people from all walks of life involved. It is particularly recommended for families with young children. When on holiday, accommodation expenses comprise a relatively large part of the holiday budget – if we can succeed in attracting people to Britain on exchange schemes, I believe that local economies can only benefit in the future.

Presenter: What else do you do to make sure that customers are satisfied?

Marion: On the last page of every catalogue, there is a questionnaire. We ask people who have been on our exchanges to fill it in and send it back to us at the end of their holiday. Take this one, for example. Let's call her Ana, from Malaga, in Spain, who has been involved in house swapping for the last four years. The first two summers she went to France, the following two summers were spent in Scotland and Holland respectively. She says that despite her initial misgivings, she now recommends it to her friends and associates. She's added that it's made her want to upgrade her own house! So, you see, we take great care to ensure that our customers are satisfied and happy with the arrangements. Her comments are from just one of the many questionnaires returned to us every season. So far, they have all been favourable and many people have suggested ways to make our service even more efficient.

Presenter: Is home swapping getting to be big business then?

Marion: Oh yes, our last catalogue contained more than 15 thousand entries! Since we started the scheme, business has increased by 20 per cent every year. We cover thirty countries in Europe and elsewhere and we are still expanding. The number of Spanish families participating in such a scheme, however, is still less than 200 so there is room for us to improve there. By the way, each client can expect to receive between 15 and 20 proposals, but not everybody wants to stay in a tourist area; often they would like to go abroad but would prefer a quiet holiday.

Presenter: Thank you, Marion.

PAUSE 10 seconds

Now you'll hear Part Three again.

TONE

REPEAT Part Three

PAUSE 5 seconds

That's the end of Part Three.

Now turn to Part Four.

PAUSE 5 seconds

Part 4

Part Four consists of two tasks.

You will hear five short extracts in which people talk about a disability or medical condition they have.

Look at Task 1. For questions 21-25 choose from the list (A-H) what challenge each speaker faced due to their condition.

Now look at Task 2. For questions 26-30 choose from the list (A-H) how their condition cause each speaker to change.

While you listen, you must complete both tasks.

You now have forty-five seconds in which to look at Part Four.

PAUSE 45 seconds

TONE

Speaker 1

PAUSE 2 seconds

Due to human growth hormone deficiency as a child, and despite some treatment, my growth was stunted and I only reached the height of 4' 9'' as an adult, which is the average height of an eleven year old. While I know there are people much worse off than me when it comes to having a medical condition, it has made some aspects of my life tiresome and difficult. I really resent having to shop for kids' clothes for myself and the thing about being the same height as a child is that lots of people then treat you like one. This is especially annoying as I'm a barrister and it means I have to be twice as strong and determined in court to make my presence felt and to be taken seriously. I've had to develop a very assertive personality to make up for my lack of stature, but luckily, one thing I don't lack is fighting spirit.

PAUSE 3 seconds

Speaker 2

PAUSE 2 seconds

Seven years ago I lost a leg in a motorbike accident. I was completely devastated at the time and it's taken me a long time to come to terms with what happened. Even now, there are times when I ask myself 'why me?',

but I know there is no answer to that question and that it's up to me to learn to live with it and get on with life or sink into a slough of self pity. Prosthetic limbs are very hi-tech these days and I have the same range of movement as anyone else, so I'm not physically limited by my disability. I still go hiking in the mountains and I play football, too. When people find out that I have a prosthetic limb they often get embarrassed and change the subject, which really irritates me, but, like everything else, I've learned to live with it. All I can do is try to educate people about my disability and show that I'm no different from anyone else.

PAUSE 3 seconds

Speaker 3

PAUSE 2 seconds

I started getting alopecia in my teens and it gradually got worse until I lost all my hair. A few wisps of hair grow back but basically, I'll probably never have a full head of hair again. Some women with alopecia learn to embrace their baldness and flaunt it. But I can't. I can't stand people staring at me. And people often mistake me for a cancer victim undergoing chemotherapy, which makes me feel even worse as apart from the hair loss, I'm perfectly healthy. So I wear a wig and I use false eyelashes, too. My husband thinks I should try not wearing a wig. He's very supportive and makes me feel good about myself. But I'm too self conscious to go out without a wig and I think most people are very judgemental and often, downright rude to people who look a little different.

PAUSE 3 seconds

Speaker 4

PAUSE 2 seconds

I was diagnosed with Asperger's when I was in my teens. It's a disorder on the autism spectrum and it means that even though I have a very high IQ, I have a problem with social interaction and understanding other people's emotions and reactions. It makes it hard for me to have social relationships and make friends. But I'm very happy working as a librarian and my colleagues and the library users have got used to me now. I think they just think I'm a bit odd, really. There's no form of treatment for Asperger's, I just have to live with it and I make sure I explain it to people when I meet them. Once people understand that I'm not being rude by not reacting to normal social cues then I usually get on fine with people.

PAUSE 3 seconds

Speaker 5

PAUSE 2 seconds

I've had multiple sclerosis for over ten years now. The thing with MS is that it probably won't kill you but it can make life very difficult. When I first started to get attacks, I could go months and months with no symptoms at all until the next attack occurred. Now I've got some permanent coordination problems and I've had to give up driving. The only thing that worries me is if the condition deteriorates further I'd have to give up my job as a bank manager. All I can do is hope that it doesn't because there's no way of knowing until it happens. Some people with MS only ever get mild symptoms and other people end up in a wheelchair.

PAUSE 10 seconds

Now you'll hear Part Four again.

TONE

REPEAT Part Four

PAUSE 5 seconds

That's the end of Part Four.

There'll now be a pause of five minutes for you to copy your answers onto the separate answer sheet. Be sure to follow the numbering of all the questions. I'll remind you when there is one minute left, so that you're sure to finish in time.

PAUSE 4 minutes

You have one more minute left.

PAUSE 1 minute

That's the end of the test. Please stop now. Your supervisor will now collect all the question papers and answer sheets.

Practice Test 4 — Paper 3 Listening

This is the Certificate of Proficiency in English Listening Test. Test 4.

I'm going to give you the instructions for this test. I'll introduce each part of the test and give you time to look at the questions.

At the start of each piece you'll hear this sound:

TONE

You'll hear each piece twice.

Remember, while you're listening, write your answers on the question paper. You'll have five minutes at the end of the test to copy your answers onto the separate answer sheet.

There will now be a pause. Please ask any questions now, because you must not speak during the test.

PAUSE 5 seconds

Part 1

Now open your question paper and look at Part One.

PAUSE 5 seconds

You will hear three different extracts. For questions 1-6, choose the answer (A, B or C) which fits best according to what you hear. There are two questions for each extract.

Extract One

PAUSE 15 seconds

TONE

Man: It's so easy for couples to quarrel, though, isn't it? You know the scenario – the husband comes home a little jaded, a little on edge. So, when something trivial isn't quite right – the dinner isn't all that good, for example – he starts complaining.
Woman: Sounds all too familiar – the wife defends herself and brings up the ridiculously small amount of money she has to run the house on and the fact that she needs a new cooker ...
Man: ... and before they know what's happening, all kinds of other things are coming up. In-laws, money, broken promises from the time before they got married, and since their marriage, anything in fact.
Woman: And, in the end nothing is settled and both sides have new ammunition to make the next quarrel even more vicious.
Man: Hmm ... there's really no way out of it except to break the cycle. Stopping and thinking about whether it's really worth it before launching into an offensive!
Woman: Yes, and very often it isn't. In fact, it's probably something you'd laugh at if you hadn't been in such a bad mood to begin with.

PAUSE 5 seconds

TONE

REPEAT Extract One

PAUSE 2 seconds

Extract Two

PAUSE 15 seconds

TONE

Man: The fire of London was the worst fire in all of the city's history. It began when an oven was inadvertently left unattended in the house of the King's baker in Pudding Lane, near London Bridge. A violent east wind encouraged the flames, which raged during the whole of Monday and part of Tuesday. On Wednesday, the fire slackened and on Thursday it was extinguished. However, on the evening of that day, the flames again burst forth at the Temple. Using gunpowder, some houses were blown up at once, and so the fire was finally mastered, leaving thousands homeless. Within a few short days of the fire, three different plans were presented to the King for the rebuilding of the city, however, none of these plans to regularise the streets was ever adopted, and, in consequence, the old street lines were in almost every case retained. Nevertheless, Wren did begin work on his greatest work, the new St. Paul's Cathedral and the many churches which ranged around it as satellites. In the 1670s, The Monument, a huge commemorative column, was erected close to the source of the blaze.

PAUSE 5 seconds

TONE

REPEAT Extract Two

PAUSE 2 seconds

Extract Three

PAUSE 15 seconds

TONE

In the six years since its opening, the Doug Carrick-designed Angus South Course has been upgraded from Best New Gold Course of the Year to the 14th Ranked Course in Canada. In fact, since its inception in 1996, the course has enjoyed overwhelming popularity and success. An unprecedented number of new members, and an influx of weekend golfers keep the finely trained staff at the course on their toes. In fact, it was this ever-increasing membership that prompted management to open the brand new Angus Glen North Course. Angus Glen South, the existing course, is a wonderful combination of natural meadows and rolling terrain, which together have created an unsurpassed championship layout. Water comes into play strategically at several holes, as the Bruce Creek flows unencumbered across the property. Sand traps, generously filled with white Ohio sand, grace the luxurious fairways and greens, adding to the challenge of the course. Whether you choose to test out your driving skills on the South Course, or your putting abilities on the new North Course, rest assured Angus Glen will provide all you golfers with an exciting and rewarding experience.

PAUSE 5 seconds

TONE

REPEAT Extract Three

PAUSE 2 seconds

That's the end of Part One.

Now turn to Part Two.

PAUSE 5 seconds

Part 2

You will hear part of a radio talk on an ancient Mesoamerican city and the discoveries that were made there. For questions 7-15, complete the sentences with a word or short phrase.

You now have forty-five seconds in which to look at Part Two.

PAUSE 45 seconds

TONE

I think I'll begin with a small preamble about the monumental ruins of Mesoamerica. This area has long been a humbling testimony to the complex civilisations that once flourished there. Even the names of these people evoke a sense of power and mystery; Aztecs, Maya, Sapotecs, Toltecs and so on. But of all the great pre-Columbian metropolises that dot the region, the most magnificent of all belonged to a people who remain nameless.

The Aztecs took over the area some, say roughly, 40 kilometres north of modern Mexico City, in as late as the 15th century. They were, of course, convinced that its city had been built by supernatural beings. The Aztec name for the city, which we still use, is Teotihuacan, which in English translates as 'Place of the Gods.'

Until the 1960s, no one realised that Teotihuacan's great Avenue of the Dead was the core of a much larger metropolis. Indeed, at 21 square kilometres and with an estimated population of 150,000, Teotihuacan was the largest city in Mesoamerica in its heyday, and one of the six largest in the world – even larger than Rome. Its political power reached all the way to Mayan city-states, with outposts as far away as Guatemala.

Unlike its Mayan counterparts, though, Teotihuacan has yielded very few inscriptions, and we have not as yet been able to decipher them. Unfortunately, the city's celebrated painted murals don't provide many clues either, so there are very few glimpses of daily life; the best information we have to date comes from a series of mass graves discovered in 1989.

Most of the 150 skeletons found there were buried facing north, suggesting some kind of ceremorial burial had taken place. Most of them had been dressed as soldiers and armed with stone tipped spears and other weapons. More skeletons were discovered within what we call the 'Pyramid of the Sun', but these discoveries only managed to raise as many questions as they answered about Teotihuacan culture. Then earlier this year, some of my colleagues and I made a fantastic find. We decided to tackle the Pyramid of the Moon. Like most Mesoamerican pyramids, this one was built like an onion; they would build a small pyramid, then build a larger one over it and then build a third one after that. This makes the interior almost solid dirt and rubble, with no distinct passageways. It makes the going slow and expensive. It took us over three months to reach the burial chamber, which is about 27 metres inside the pyramid but it was worth the trouble. No one has ever found a burial of this richness intact at Teotihuacan before. As well as a skeleton, we found, amongst other items, statuettes, at least 15 double edged knives, some pyrite discs which served as mirrors, the remnants of a wooden cage and the skeletons of large cats and some birds.

But it was the human remains that had my attention. Once they have been fully extricated, we will try to determine the individual's age and gender. We will also look for evidence of disease, malnutrition or developmental abnormalities as well as wounds, broken limbs or signs of hard labour and such status symbols as filed teeth. Initially, we thought the individual might have been a ruler or a person of high status, but it may not turn out like that considering that the person, who was probably male, doesn't seem to have any lavish body ornaments.

The real key to unravelling the secrets of Teotihuacan is more digging – a lot more. Our team is still hard at work. Despite this impressive discovery, 95 per cent of the city is still unexcavated. We're scratching the surface.

PAUSE 10 seconds

Now you'll hear Part Two again.

TONE

REPEAT Part Two

PAUSE 5 seconds

That's the end of Part Two.

Now turn to Part Three.

PAUSE 5 seconds

Part 3

You will hear an interview with Jack Taylor, the creator of the very popular cartoon character, Carla. For questions 16-20, choose the answer (A, B, C or D) which best fits what you hear.

You now have one minute in which to look at Part Three.

PAUSE 1 minute

TONE

Interviewer: Anyone surprised that a twenty-five-year-old children's character could suddenly become a global phenomenon has nothing on Jack Taylor, the creator of Carla, that distinctive 8-year-old, all-too human crocodile. Jack, welcome to the show.

Jack: Thanks Pat, it's a pleasure to be here. As you said before, no one is more shocked than myself at Carla's unexpected success. It just amazes me, and puzzles me, that so many kids and their families could have related so strongly to this unlikely character, I mean she is a crocodile after all.

Interviewer: Jack, where did Carla originate from?

Jack: I can thank my daughter for Carla. One evening at bedtime, she complained that she was bored with the same old stories every night and asked me to make something up. Well, we had just been to the zoo, so I made up some story about a crocodile and she loved it. Clara's personality built up slowly, and her life often developed to reflect my daughter's life. For example, when my daughter started having swimming lessons, Carla also ditched her armbands and had a go at swimming by herself. Of course, Carla isn't the only character and her older brother Andrew was a central character of the stories from very early on, and naturally he corresponds to my son.

Interviewer: Can you give us a few details about Carla's long path to success?

Jack: Of course. In the beginning, it looked as if Carla was attractive and endearing only to my daughter. When the first Carla book, 'Carla's Wobbly Tooth', was published in 1988, I made the grand total of £190 in royalties in the first six months. My publisher suggested that I raised interest by touring the country, visiting schools and reading Carla stories to the children. It was their excitement and enjoyment of the characters that made me persevere with the series, even when my daughter had completely outgrown the stories.

Interviewer: Do the stories only appeal to girls, or can boys enjoy them too?

Jack: The title character is, of course, female and that was very important for me as I believe that there aren't enough strong female characters in children's fiction. While she does have a girlie side, she loves adventure, is fiercely competitive and holds her own in the company of her brother and his friends. Some boys, of course, will never touch a book with a female title character, but the stories are really about Andrew as much as Carla. I think the thrills and irritations that come from having an older brother, or a younger sister, are ones that many girls and boys can relate to.

Interviewer: What triggered the character's overnight propulsion into the limelight?

Jack: It came out of the blue. One afternoon, I had just finished an appearance and I was approached by Rebecca Harris, who introduced herself as a producer. She asked me if I'd be willing to work on an animated series starring Carla. Of course, I jumped at the chance but I never expected the show to be such a success, nor that it would also gain large audiences when shown abroad. I think it has a broad appeal, and it has even gained a following among adults who love the humour of the show. There was a lot of interest in the characters, and I had no objections when the production company suggested bringing out the range of merchandise. And now here we are and the Carla and Andrew stuffed toys are this year's must-haves for Christmas.

Interviewer: Does it bother you that interest in the toys and TV show has eclipsed that of your books?

Jack: Well, you're right that the toys and the TV show are selling more than my books ever did. But more and more kids are turning to the books to learn more about the characters and their exploits, and at the moment the books are flying off the shelves. With the TV show and merchandising, I've managed to reach a huge audience, and if just a small percentage of those turn to my books and discover a love of reading, I will feel very satisfied.

PAUSE 10 seconds

Now you'll hear Part Three again.

TONE

REPEAT Part Three

PAUSE 5 seconds

That's the end of Part Three.

Now turn to Part Four.

PAUSE 5 seconds

Part 4

Part Four consists of two tasks.

You will hear five short extracts in which people talk about the role technology plays in their life.

Look at Task 1. For questions 21-25 choose from the list (A-H) what each person says about how technology has affected their life.

Now look at Task 2. For questions 26-30 choose from the list (A-H) how each person's attitude towards technology has changed.

You will hear the recording twice. While you listen, you must complete both tasks.

You now have forty-five seconds in which to look at Part Four.

PAUSE 45 seconds

TONE

Speaker 1

PAUSE 2 seconds

When I think back to my youth and remember how we thought a black and white television was an incredible hi-tech development, it seems funny now. Up until I retired, I didn't really have much use for any gadgets and I thought it would be too much like hard work to learn how to use them. But living on my own, I'd be very lonely if I didn't have the internet and a decent mobile. I can keep in touch with friends and relatives using my mobile wherever I am and I like using my laptop to chat to people on Skype. It's great that I can see the people I'm chatting to as well as hear them. And it really wasn't that hard to learn how to use the technology. It's so user friendly that there's nothing to be scared of even if you've never used it before.

PAUSE 3 seconds

Speaker 2

PAUSE 2 seconds

With each new advancement in technology I get a massive rush of excitement about what kind of difference it will make to me as a wheelchair user. I'm always hopeful that some breakthrough will come along and completely change my life. But I've had to learn to accept that although developments do make a difference to me, and have made life easier, they will never really change the basic fact that I'm in a wheelchair and I can't be 100% independent. It's just something I've had to come to terms with over the years. But that's not to say that things aren't easier now than they were ten years ago. My wheelchair itself is a brilliant design and a dream to use. And I can do so much more around the house on my own these days because of the equipment I have had installed.

PAUSE 3 seconds

Speaker 3

PAUSE 2 seconds

I really think that we've become too reliant on technology and that this is damaging to society on many levels. It's changing people's relationships and its destroying our connection with nature and the environment. I used to be really into having top of the range gear like a smartphone, a tablet, games consoles, you name it. But it was gradually taking over my life. Then, while I was at uni, I had a bit of an epiphany and decided to make a stand against the encroaching machines. I had to totally change every aspect of my lifestyle and my values. Now I run an organic farm and I try to keep my life as gadget free as possible. I also lecture on the dangers that an over reliance on technology poses for human society and point out that it's retrogressive and not an evolution at all, as far as I'm concerned.

PAUSE 3 seconds

Speaker 4

PAUSE 2 seconds

Different types of technology have sort of crept into my life unawares. For years, mobile phones and computers were something my kids used, or my husband. But then I found I enjoyed using the internet for all sorts of things. Looking up information, taking part in blogs, social networking, buying goods online. I even run my own blog now. It's about being a stay at home mum. I've got readers from all over the world who comment on the blog and now I tweet about my blog and I've got a Facebook group too. I'm surprised how much fun the new technology is and it's really improved my level of contact with people. I've just bought a new smartphone and my husband has promised me a tablet for my birthday. It's great learning all the ways you can make the most of these advances. Technology isn't just for the very young!

PAUSE 3 seconds

Speaker 5

PAUSE 2 seconds

I run a business that operates in many parts of the world. We manufacture parts for computers, smart phones and HD TVs. The equipment in our factories is the latest in robotics technology and much of the way we market and distribute goods is heavily reliant on a wide range of hi-tech networks. I've always believed in the development of technology but I had expected it to slow down in the noughties, that markets would reach saturation and a platform would be reached because of consumer fatigue. But with so much innovation going on and so much more societal reliance on staying 'connected' in a variety of ways, the market is just expanding exponentially for hi-tech goods. I can see it in my own life. I'm a high powered executive and I spend a lot of time on the road or jetting across the world. Connectivity is very important. I need to be in constant contact with

colleagues and clients. Imagine what it would be like trying to do all that nowadays with nothing more than a fax and a landline!

PAUSE 10 seconds

Now you'll hear Part Four again.

TONE

REPEAT Part Four

PAUSE 5 seconds

That's the end of Part Four.

There'll now be a pause of five minutes for you to copy your answers onto the separate answer sheet. Be sure to follow the numbering of all the questions. I'll remind you when there is one minute left, so that you're sure to finish in time.

PAUSE 4 minutes

You have one more minute left.

PAUSE 1 minute

That's the end of the test. Please stop now. Your supervisor will now collect all the question papers and answer sheets.

Practice Test 5 — Paper 3 Listening

This is the Certificate of Proficiency in English Listening Test. Test 5.

I'm going to give you the instructions for this test. I'll introduce each part of the test and give you time to look at the questions.

At the start of each piece you'll hear this sound:

TONE

You'll hear each piece twice.

Remember, while you're listening, write your answers on the question paper. You'll have five minutes at the end of the test to copy your answers onto the separate answer sheet.

There will now be a pause. Please ask any questions now, because you must not speak during the test.

PAUSE 5 seconds

Part 1

Now open your question paper and look at Part One.

PAUSE 5 seconds

You will hear three different extracts. For questions 1-6, choose the answer (A, B or C) which fits best according to what you hear. There are two questions for each extract.

Extract One

PAUSE 15 seconds

TONE

Woman: What brought me here in the first place? Pure chance really. After my husband died, I needed some time and space to work out my future. Running away really. I found myself in this valley, oh, fifteen years ago, now, as a curious observer backpacking through.

Seeing the poverty that was here at close quarters really made me stop and think. I really felt for these poor people and wanted to do something to help them. That's how I got involved.

Leprosy is a big problem here, and even though it's easy to treat and is curable, many people hide the signs and symptoms for fear of being ostracised. By then of course, the disease has done its damage and the lepers are reduced to begging in the streets.

I live a simple life. I will never give it up, well, not willingly, anyway.

PAUSE 5 seconds

TONE

REPEAT Extract One

PAUSE 2 seconds

Extract Two

PAUSE 15 seconds

TONE

James: Well, I think it's important that we should provide training for these young people.

Allison: Why should we? They all went to school didn't they? Or at least they should have done, but I expect those that slipped through the net skipped school. It was their choice!

James: Not always. Some of these youngsters need to feel that they are valued by society, not constantly put down. And being illiterate makes it very difficult to find employment. That's why a lot of them turned to crime in the first place.

Allison: Half of these kids were delinquents to start with. That's really why they missed out on their schooling.

James: But wouldn't it be better if we tried to put things right while they're here, ... it would give them a feeling that they had something to offer?

Allison: OK, but I still think you're being a bit soft on them. What they need is a short, sharp shock.

James: That formula has been tried but it didn't really work. We have to stop thinking that these kids are here for more punishment. Just being here is the punishment; they're here to be rehabilitated and education is part of that.

PAUSE 5 seconds

TONE

REPEAT Extract Two

PAUSE 2 seconds

Extract Three

PAUSE 15 seconds

TONE

Man: Relics and underwater video film of what are believed to be the ancient Egyptian cities of Herakleion and Menouthis, which lie in Aboukir Bay off Alexandria, were shown for the first time this month. Tell us more.

Woman: The cities were submerged more than 1,000 years ago, probably by seismic activity, and although classical Greek writings mention them, there had been little tangible evidence until this discovery.

Man: Apart from the obvious reasons, what makes this find special?

Woman: We are used to finding the remains of a tomb, a church or mosque. This time we are finding complete cities. The area around Alexandria is rich in land-based archaeological treasures. Millions of people live on top of the ancient remains, which are about 12 metres below street level. In fact, some relics have almost certainly been destroyed by the foundations of modern buildings. The difficulty of working on land has led archaeologists to the sea. The water is shallow and the ruins, relatively untouched, lie as little as 5 metres below the surface, covered by a thin layer of sand.

PAUSE 5 seconds

TONE

REPEAT Extract Three

PAUSE 2 seconds

That's the end of Part One.

Now turn to Part Two.

PAUSE 5 seconds

Part 2

You will hear a radio documentary about myths. For questions 7-15, complete the sentences with a word or short phrase.

You now have forty-five seconds in which to look at Part Two.

PAUSE 45 seconds

TONE

Presenter: I can remember, as a child, being fascinated by the exploits of the many gods and demi-gods found in Greek mythology. As I grew older, I came to the realisation that myth-making was almost invariably a universal practice. Today, Dave McDuff, a professor of sociology at Trinity College, is going to take to us on some interesting aspects of myths and mythology. Professor McDuff.

McDuff: The myths were the first creation of the human mind, and they were formed out of a deep need to put living things into a logical system. The awe that man experienced when faced by the uncontrollable forces of nature, his anxieties, his awareness both of his weakness and uniqueness, and even the moral beliefs on which he based his own life and his communication with his fellow human beings – all these were expressed in narratives with a symbolic content. The myths provide us with a clear picture of how each group of people differed, of the way they thought, of their achievements and of their course through history.

The Ancient Greeks were among the earliest peoples to create myths, which they considered to be a way of understanding and interpreting anything which struck them as inexplicable and impossible to control. Their narratives were passed down orally from generation to generation, changing and becoming richer according to the needs of each era. The Greeks combined their mythological traditions with their wealth of moral concepts in order to produce a series of supreme beings, the gods, who commanded the universe and ordered human destiny. These gods were the object of their worship, and divine conduct was their guide in deciding how to live a virtuous life. The feats of the gods and heroes were a source of inspiration and creation for the Greeks, leading them on the upward path that led to the reaching of ambitious goals. Mythology stimulated the restless minds of the Greeks, and was the force that led to the creating of what today we call Greek civilisation.

The first consideration to which the Greeks – like all the other peoples of the world – gave their attention was that of how the world was created and of the powers that controlled its operation. The earliest inhabitants seemed to have identified the universe with the Earth itself. The fertility of nature and the fruitfulness both of the Earth and of mankind were seen as the ultimate mysteries, and deified. The Earth, with its creative powers, took the form of a female deity, who was responsible for fertility and reproduction. The prehistoric inhabitants of Greece worshipped this goddess in sacred places, depicted her in art and honoured her with offerings. It wasn't until the Mycenean period, that the great Earth goddess was flanked by a whole host of new deities, most of them male. Thanks to the deciphering of the ancient texts we know that this was the time that saw the birth of the gods whose names have survived until today in ancient Greek mythology. The names of Zeus, Ares, Hermes, Dionysus and Poseidon, who were the most important gods of that period, have been read and inscribed on clay tablets found in the Mycenean palaces.

PAUSE 10 seconds

Now you'll hear Part Two again.

TONE

REPEAT Part Two

PAUSE 5 seconds

That's the end of Part Two.

Now turn to Part Three.

PAUSE 5 seconds

Part 3

You will hear an interview with Margery Paige, a specialist in alternative medicine. For questions 16-20, choose the answer (A, B, C or D) which best fits what you hear.

You now have one minute in which to look at Part Three.

PAUSE 1 minute

TONE

Interviewer: Someone who recently attended a rather unusual convention, which took place in Somerset last weekend, is Margery Paige, who most of us know from her weekly newspaper column on alternative therapies, and who has just returned from the first annual Alternative Mind Convention. Margery, this is the first convention of its type to be held here, can you fill us in on some of the background to the event?

Margery: Well, I think that among those of us who subscribe to the belief that there are more ways to treat ailments of the mind and body than the generally accepted medical methods, there had been a general feeling for some time that what was needed was some kind of formalized international forum which would be open to all those interested in alternative therapies, either as practitioners or as laymen wanting to know more. We needed to be able to meet each other and to discuss the ways in which we differ and are alike – very much like a conventional medical conference, in fact, except that in accordance with our greater transparency, if you like, we made the proceedings open to the general public as well.

Interviewer: And how did the public respond? Did you find that non-practitioners, or even perhaps some sceptics did attend, or were you preaching to the converted?

Margery: No, not at all. I must admit I was surprised to see how many people made the journey down to the conference centre just out of interest. In a sense, it made the proceedings more valuable, since if a speaker has to address a group of people who may not necessarily be familiar with what he or she does, then assumptions about what they know can't be made; one has to define terms and processes much more precisely. It avoided the fuzzy thinking of which we are often accused.

Interviewer: I see. Did you find that the people who attended showed particular interest in any one area?

Margery: Not really, I don't think so. There was the usual amount of interest shown in the Chinese idea of the Yin and Yang qualities in our lives, or the darkness and light that revolve around the 'Ch'i' or energy that surrounds us. The idea here being that any impediment to the flow of this energy will cause an imbalance and therefore an illness of some kind. It's an idea that attracts a great many people. Oh, and surprisingly enough, a great interest in colour therapy, which is based on the notion that colours have an effect on the mind and the body; how they can be used to alter mood, for example, such as on the effects of colour in the workplace.

Interviewer: Yes, indeed. Margery, if you had to sum the conference up, what would you say were the main gains for the world of alternative medicine?

Margery: Difficult one. Well, I think we are all aware that proponents of alternative medical treatments have had to struggle hard against traditional medicine's view that we were just a lot of cranks, so it was heartening to see that there is a clear common trend in alternative therapies, from whichever part of the world they come. The idea of psychological health being closely allied to physical health is a strong one, and of course the central concept of a holistic view. Still more interesting was the fact that

there were a fair number of medical doctors there, which would indicate that more and more conventional medical practitioners are becoming sympathetic to many of the alternative treatments, so I think we will soon see the day when the two approaches to health will come together.

Interviewer: That'll be a day to look forward to. Margery Paige, thank you for coming to talk to us. If listeners would like further information on the subject they can contact ... *(fade)*

PAUSE 10 seconds

Now you'll hear Part Three again.

TONE

REPEAT Part Three

PAUSE 5 seconds

That's the end of Part Three.

Now turn to Part Four.

PAUSE 5 seconds

Part 4

Part Four consists of two tasks.

You will hear five short extracts in which people talk about how they spend their free time.

Look at Task 1. For questions 21-25 choose from the list (A-H) what the profession of each speaker is.

Now look at Task 2. For questions 26-30 choose from the list (A-H) which best summarises what each person feels about their leisure time.

You will hear the recording twice. While you listen, you must complete both tasks.

You now have forty-five seconds in which to look at Part Four.

PAUSE 45 seconds

TONE

Speaker 1

PAUSE 2 seconds

Because of my work, a lot of my free time involves entertaining clients for the company. Taking them out to dinner, or arranging an evening at the opera. Anything that is likely to be both congenial and likely to impress the clients. Especially the overseas ones. It's a very good way of getting people into a receptive frame of mind and really does help me to close a lot of my deals to the company's benefit. So, I don't mind sacrificing a slice of my private life if it really helps the company go forward. Apart from that, what little spare free time I have is spent with my family.

Mainly at weekends, if I'm not needed for a foreign trip.

PAUSE 3 seconds

Speaker 2

PAUSE 2 seconds

During the week, by the time I've shut up the shop and sorted everything out it's usually gone 9pm. As I live alone and the dog is stuck indoors all day, I usually take her for a late turn round the neighbourhood. On the weekend, I shut up early on Saturday and I've my own shopping to do for the week, mainly groceries, of course, and then a quiet night in. As Sundays are my only full day off, I try to make a day of it. I might take a trip to visit friends or relatives. Or even invite friends round for a good meal. I want my Sundays to be as fun filled as possible as Monday morning I have to get to the shop early to deal with suppliers, organise staff rotas and a thousand other jobs to boot.

PAUSE 3 seconds

Speaker 3

PAUSE 2 seconds

Free time is something I may have to defer for a few more years until I've established myself better. At the moment I'm simply eating, sleeping and breathing the fashion world. And it's a cut-throat business. Take your eye off the ball and you might find that you've been replaced as creative director by someone younger and keener, who is willing to work every hour of the night or day to get a collection together. I do go out to dinner with friends quite a lot. And the fashion world has lots of corporate events and promotions where everyone gets dressed up and goes for cocktails or something. But that's as much a part of work as organising a show. I do take a summer holiday every year, though, and think myself lucky for those blessed two quick weeks!

PAUSE 3 seconds

Speaker 4

PAUSE 2 seconds

Most evenings a week I get home and just flop in front of the TV. People think that clerical work isn't tiring because there's not much physical exertion. But it's exhausting staring at a computer screen all day. At the end of the week, my colleagues and I will all go out for coffee to unwind after all the hard slog we've put in. My weekends are spent catching up with housework in the flat, tidying up and sorting out laundry, as well as seeing friends. We might go out or we'll all pile round one person's house for the

evening. Sundays, I usually go to visit my parents for a couple of hours and then I go to the gym for a good long work out as it's the only chance I get.

PAUSE 3 seconds

Speaker 5

PAUSE 2 seconds

The work I do requires a great deal of concentration and the results could help save lives. Generally, the mornings I spend in the lab are very labour intensive and once I've written up a preliminary report, I'll take the rest of the day off. But even when I'm relaxing, my pursuits tend to be intellectual rather than physical. I enjoy long deep novels that I can lose myself in entirely and I play a lot of chess. Apart from the chess club, I'm not much of a socialiser. I find people too garrulous but with nothing to say. I enjoy quiet and contemplative activities. They replenish my energy much more than running around from party to party like some people do.

PAUSE 10 seconds

Now you'll hear Part Four again.

TONE

REPEAT Part Four

PAUSE 5 seconds

That's the end of Part Four.

There'll now be a pause of five minutes for you to copy your answers onto the separate answer sheet. Be sure to follow the numbering of all the questions. I'll remind you when there is one minute left, so that you're sure to finish in time.

PAUSE 4 minutes

You have one more minute left.

PAUSE 1 minute

That's the end of the test. Please stop now. Your supervisor will now collect all the question papers and answer sheets.

Practice Test 6 — Paper 3 Listening

This is the Certificate of Proficiency in English Listening Test. Test 6.

I'm going to give you the instructions for this test. I'll introduce each part of the test and give you time to look at the questions.

At the start of each piece you'll hear this sound:

TONE

You'll hear each piece twice.

Remember, while you're listening, write your answers on the question paper. You'll have five minutes at the end of the test to copy your answers onto the separate answer sheet.

There will now be a pause. Please ask any questions now, because you must not speak during the test.

PAUSE 5 seconds

Part 1

Now open your question paper and look at Part One.

PAUSE 5 seconds

You will hear three different extracts. For questions 1-6, choose the answer (A, B or C) which fits best according to what you hear. There are two questions for each extract.

Extract One

PAUSE 15 seconds

TONE

Man: The 20 directors I chose as my subjects reflect a wide range of backgrounds and sensibilities. Yet no matter where one hails from, a chance to direct requires a good script, singleness of purpose bordering on monomania and more than a fair share of luck.
Woman: I liked the first-hand accounts. They were interesting.
Man: Yes, and I was touched by stories of the director overcoming a moment of such hopelessness that a weaker soul might have thrown up his hands and left the business altogether.
Woman: It's quite a technical book isn't it ... who do you think it will appeal to?
Man: Oh ... any lover of film really, it is also well-suited to the needs of novice filmmakers and should provide them with hope and inspiration ... also disabuse them of the all too prevalent notion that filmmaking is a one-person job. It is a collaborative medium and there is no shame in depending on the talent of others.

PAUSE 5 seconds

TONE

REPEAT Extract One

PAUSE 2 seconds

Extract Two

PAUSE 15 seconds

TONE

Man: The mountainous character of the island ensures that driving is a leisurely process, as you wind through a seemingly endless series of hairpin bends. It is just as well, because the car occasionally has some unusual hazards to negotiate. Coming round the corner, we were suddenly confronted by a large rock inching its way across our path.
We stopped to inspect and found it wasn't a rock but a living fossil, a beast as old as the dinosaurs themselves, which had chosen that moment to cross our path. It felt like an honour. In fact, when the wild tortoise started to emerge from its shell, pushing paddle-like limbs down on the asphalt to renew its journey, we were moved by a double sense of privilege. It appeared to know we intended no harm, and with that sad, ancient eloquence the skeletal head turned in our direction to acknowledge our presence. Then the rock continued on its course and we were left to reflect on its message.

PAUSE 5 seconds

TONE

REPEAT Extract Two

PAUSE 2 seconds

Extract Three

PAUSE 15 seconds

TONE

Thinning hair, accumulating body fat, dissatisfaction at the way life has panned out ... the signs of a mid-life crisis are clear, but as booming sales in the premium cycling market testify, rather than following the stereotype and hankering after a sports car in their quest to rediscover their youth, British men today often splash their cash on a racing bike. Given Britain's recent success in professional cycling, this is hardly surprising. For those inspired by Sir Chris Hoy and Sir Bradley Wiggins, the appeal is clear: the chance to emulate your heroes, to swap harsh reality for the open road and to burn off some of that excess fat in the process. This is good news for retailers such as Halfords, who recently announced plans to increase their stock of specialist bikes, but bad news for teenage sons and daughters, for whom the sight of dad in Lycra, beer-belly and all, may outweigh the thrill of a spin on his new bike. And if your husband blows ten grand on a Pinarello Dogma 2, currently the last word in bicycle engineering, be thankful - it's still only a fraction of the cost of a sports car.

PAUSE 5 seconds

TONE

REPEAT Extract Three

PAUSE 2 seconds

That's the end of Part One.

Now turn to Part Two.

PAUSE 5 seconds

Part 2

You will hear part of a radio feature where a woman talks about how she copes with migraine attacks. For questions 7-15, complete the sentences with a word or short phrase.

You now have forty-five seconds in which to look at Part Two.

PAUSE 45 seconds

TONE

Presenter: In this week's 'Healthy Living' we are going to hear Sharon Stevens talking about a very common ailment called migraine and how she copes with it. Sharon, just how do you cope with migraine? I had an attack once and I was unable to work for days!

Sharon: Well, it all depends on the type of attacks you get. There are two main types of migraine, common and classical migraine. The common variety involves a severe one-sided headache that may last for several days. These are sometimes called 'sick headaches'. There are several very effective treatments nowadays, but the important thing is to take the medication as soon as the symptoms manifest themselves. Classical migraine, the type I have, is different and involves a variety of symptoms, not just a headache. Sometimes, long before a headache develops, there are visual disturbances. I may be watching TV when suddenly everything to the left is blotted out. Soon after, everything to the right is jumbled up, just like a kaleidoscope! ... The first time it happened, I was very frightened but I was only eight years old at the time ... This lasts for about twenty minutes and during this time, I get very confused and often mix up my words. At the same time, I get a feeling of pins and needles all down one side. These symptoms are very similar to that of a stroke and of course, can easily be mistaken for one if you can't explain that it is only a migraine. It's important that you let your colleagues know that you are subject to these attacks, especially if, as in my case, you don't get them that often. I'm lucky that I get such a long warning of an attack so that I am able to take medication in order to ward off the headache, which, if untreated, can be excruciatingly painful. Migraine can be quite distressing but the good thing is the benign nature of the condition. That is to say, nobody ever died from it ..., but a stroke can be life threatening so it's important to know the difference. Certain things are known to trigger an attack and the 'triggers' can vary from instant coffee to certain food items such as cheese, or even lentils! If you can identify a trigger, you're lucky – just avoid that particular food and you'll avoid an attack. I've never been able to identify what my trigger is; it just seems to strike at random. Some people find that it's related to stress. Others find that when stress is relieved – that's when they get an attack. That type of attack is called slump migraine. I'm very lucky because after a year-long course of therapy, I only get one or two attacks a year, and the ones that I do get are very much attenuated and nowhere near as ferocious as they used to be. There are several self-help groups that deal with migraine and of course, there is a wealth of information on the Internet.

Presenter: Thank you Sharon. Next week we will be discussing accidents in the home – where most accidents happen and how they can be avoided ...

PAUSE 10 seconds

Now you'll hear Part Two again.

TONE

REPEAT Part Two

PAUSE 5 seconds

That's the end of Part Two.

Now turn to Part Three.

PAUSE 5 seconds

Part 3

You will hear an interview with Dr Timothy Cowey, a palaeontologist, who is discussing a forthcoming excavation. For questions 16-20, choose the answer (A, B, C or D) which best fits what you hear.

You now have one minute in which to look at Part Three.

PAUSE 1 minute

TONE

Interviewer: I'm proud to welcome here today the very distinguished Dr Timothy Cowey. As most of you are probably aware, Dr Cowey has recently been awarded the prestigious Bismark Prize for his work on fossils. Dr Cowey, it's a pleasure to have you with us.

Dr Cowey: Thank you.

Interviewer: I was hoping that today you could give

us some information about your coming trip to Mongolia.

Dr Cowey: Right. I must say, I'm very excited about the excavation. I've been on many digs in my day, but for someone like myself, this is a fascinating area. As you probably know, this is our second expedition and we will be working in collaboration with leading palaeontologists from Mongolia. Actually, Mongolia's Gobi desert is one of the world's most important fossil sites and we've planned excavations in two important areas: the Nemegat Basin and the 'Flaming Cliffs'.

Interviewer: The 'Flaming Cliffs'? That's an intriguing name. Is there any significance to it?

Dr Cowey: Yes, it's a name which catches the attention, isn't it? To me, it's one of the most beautiful places in the world. Very suitably named indeed. The first time I visited the area, it took my breath away. You see, the cliffs are made primarily of sandstone ... even during the day, they are a wonderful sight, but at night ... er ... in the evening ... well, I have not words to describe it. When the sun hits the cliffs, they literally glow. It's the most unimaginably brilliant orange. It only lasts for a few moments, which is part of the magic really. On another level, the Flaming Cliffs are renowned, at least by palaeontologists, as one of the best sources of fossils on the face of the earth. As a matter of fact, it was here that Roy Chapham Andres and his expedition team discovered the first nest of dinosaur eggs that the modern world had ever seen.

Interviewer: Which brings us to the fossils themselves. What are you hoping to find on this trip?

Dr Cowey: Well ... more dinosaur eggs wouldn't go amiss! No, no ... not really ... What I'm interested in is birds and over the last few years, I've been working on the evolution of birds and what fossils can tell us about how birds became flighted creatures, which, of course, they weren't originally. Wings and feathers slowly evolved, probably as an evolutionary response to an increasingly hostile environment. From fossilised remains, we have been able to trace this development and observe the changes that occurred in small animals as they took to the air. I'm hoping that this trip will yield more information and enable us to shed more light on some as yet unresolved questions.

Interviewer: Fascinating. Dr Cowey, one more question. Is this expedition open to professionals only?

Dr Cowey: On the contrary. We're hoping with this expedition to catch the attention of would-be palaeontologists from around the globe. They'll have the opportunity to work side by side with some of the

best in the field. Because of the quality of the sites, you know, there were some extremely significant finds made there during the expedition in 2000, we're managed to attract a group of the world's finest scholars and professionals. This excavation has also aroused a lot of interest because we'll be digging in other areas of Mongolia which, to date, have never been explored. We've got our hope pinned on Hongoryn Els, which is an unbelievable place with some of the highest sand dunes in the world.

Interviewer: Well, Dr Cowey, it's been very interesting talking to you and we wish you the best of luck in ...

PAUSE 10 seconds

Now you'll hear Part Three again.

TONE

REPEAT Part Three

PAUSE 5 seconds

That's the end of Part Three.

Now turn to Part Four.

PAUSE 5 seconds

Part 4

Part Four consists of two tasks.

You will hear five short extracts in which teachers talk about their job.

Look at Task 1. For questions 21-25 choose from the list (A-H) what aspect of their job each teacher particularly enjoys.

Now look at Task 2. For questions 26-30 choose from the list (A-H) what negative aspect of the job each teacher mentions.

You will hear the recording twice. While you listen, you must complete both tasks.

You now have forty-five seconds in which to look at Part Four.

PAUSE 45 seconds

TONE

Speaker 1

PAUSE 2 seconds

One of the things I like most about teaching is that it keeps you feeling youthful. Every day I get to spend my time with people who have a fresh take on life. Unlike many of my friends who are chained to their offices, I stay in touch with the trends and attitudes which are shaping the next generation. I like to think it's a two-way thing: I learn things from my students, that they, hopefully, encounter new possibilities and ways of thinking about things through me. Having said all that, those office-bound friends I mentioned are better rewarded financially. I suppose that's only to be expected when you're following your vocation!

PAUSE 3 seconds

Speaker 2

PAUSE 2 seconds

When I was young, there was one teacher who really inspired me. Till then, I had always found Physics daunting because of the maths involved. This teacher saw my potential, and showed me that equations needn't be perplexing. There's a beautiful simplicity in the way they describe the world. Without him, I would never have developed my love of science. If I can be a similar influence to some of my students, I will have achieved something as a teacher. It can be tough though! After teaching at school all day, I still have homework to mark and lessons to prepare in the evening. There's always more to be done!

PAUSE 3 seconds

Speaker 3

PAUSE 2 seconds

I have always been academically minded, and in my subject, history, you have a limited number of career options if you want to stay involved after you graduate. This is why teaching's ideal for me. I teach classes about a variety of different periods, and the syllabuses are always changing. So are the students, and they always have new questions and ideas which mean you never stand still; you're always developing, gaining different insights. The downside is that some students just do not see the point in attending class and make little effort, no matter how hard I try to engage them. It's really disheartening.

PAUSE 3 seconds

Speaker 4

PAUSE 2 seconds

I worked as an accountant for twelve years before I decided to quit and become a teacher. It was dreadfully dull. Sometimes, I barely spoke to another person for days on end. Now, I get to mix with a diverse range of people throughout my day: students of different backgrounds and ages; colleagues with a passion and drive for their subject. No day is the same, and you never return home feeling isolated. That's not to say that there's nothing tedious about teaching. Constantly having to prepare students for tests is dispiriting. Time spent going through practice papers means less time to engage the students with something interesting.

PAUSE 3 seconds

Speaker 5

PAUSE 2 seconds

I believe everyone should have the opportunity to fulfil their potential. At my school, many kids don't get the support they need at home. It's my role to give them a place where they can feel secure and develop into responsible adults. For some, it's enough that they stay off the streets and out of the gangs, but I want to encourage them and show them what's possible. I don't expect every parent to understand but I am still shocked by some of their attitudes. Yesterday, I spoke to the mother of a boy who shouted abuse at me in class, and she shrugged as if to say 'What do you expect me to do about it?'

PAUSE 10 seconds

Now you'll hear Part Four again.

TONE

REPEAT Part Four

PAUSE 5 seconds

That's the end of Part Four.

There'll now be a pause of five minutes for you to copy your answers onto the separate answer sheet. Be sure to follow the numbering of all the questions. I'll remind you when there is one minute left, so that you're sure to finish in time.

PAUSE 4 minutes

You have one more minute left.

PAUSE 1 minute

That's the end of the test. Please stop now. Your supervisor will now collect all the question papers and answer sheets.

ISBN 978-1-4715-0759-5

Express Publishing

SCHOLASTIC Phonics

Nap, Sid!

Can you spot the cat on 4 pages?

Published in the UK by Scholastic Education, 2021
Book End, Range Road, Witney, Oxfordshire, OX29 0YD
Scholastic Ireland, 89E Lagan Road, Dublin Industrial Estate, Glasnevin, Dublin, D11 HP5F

SCHOLASTIC and associated logos are trademarks and/or registered trademarks of Scholastic Inc.
www.scholastic.co.uk
© 2021 Scholastic Limited
1 2 3 4 5 6 7 8 9   1 2 3 4 5 6 7 8 9 0

Printed by Ashford Colour Press
Paper made from wood grown in sustainable forests and other controlled sources.

A CIP catalogue record for this book is available from the British Library.

ISBN 978-0702-30864-2

Author
Catherine Baker
Editorial team
Rachel Morgan, Tracy Kewley, Liz Evans
Design team
Dipa Mistry, We Are Grace
Illustrations
Kevin Payne

The mat is in.

3

tip

Retell the story